Japanese Militarism

Past and Present

Harold Hakwon Sunoo

Japanese Militarism

Past and Present

Nelson-Hall nh Chicago

Library of Congress Cataloging in Publication Data

Sŏnu, Hak-wŏn.
Japanese militarism, past and present.

1. Militarism—Japan. 2. Japan—Foreign relations—United States. 3. United States—Foreign relations—Japan. 4. Japan—History—20th century. I. Title.
JX1961.J3S66 355.02'13'0952 74-23366
ISBN: 0-88229-217-X

Manufactured in the United States of America

To

my wife, Sonia, who helped and inspired.

Contents

Preface

Japanese society today remains semifeudal from a social point of view, in spite of her miraculous economic development during the postwar era.

Japan is once again becoming a military power, a phenomenon that started out slowly enough, but during the fiscal year 1972–1973, an alarming increase of 22 percent over the previous year was evident in the military budget. The present Japanese constitution, of course, clearly prohibits rearmament, a condition imposed by the Allied Powers after defeat of Japan in World War II.

Interestingly enough, the Japanese rearmament program has been greatly encouraged by the United States government although popular sentiment among the majority of Japanese is against war. The rearmament of Japan has been closely associated with the American Pacific Defense strategy since the days of the occupation. It is this close cooperation between the two nations that has rebuilt the strong armed forces of Japan today. Contrary to the once cooperative posture on rearmament, there are now serious conflicts between Japan and America in the field of business. As an example, current American policy is to control exports of Japanese textile goods to the United States by limiting the annual increase to no more than 5 percent. Thus cooperation and competition coexist as far as Japan's relationship with the United States is concerned. Historically, conflict over business interests had brought about the first Pacific conflict.

How long will Japan continue to remain patient as a junior partner of the United States? How will Japan react to America during a crisis such as that involving oil in 1973–1974? On March 17, 1974, the Japanese government authorized an increase in the domestic price of oil products on an average of 62 percent to prevent a decline in crude oil supplies.

On the occasion of the increase, Nakasone Yasuhiro, minister of international trade and industry and the former director-general of the defense agency, who has referred to Korea as "Japan's advance stronghold," commented on the necessity of the price increase in view of the international situation. Nakasone is an important member of Tanaka's cabinet as he has been in the previous cabinets of Sato and others. Nakasone advocates building nuclear weapons in Japan independently. It is probable that such weapons will be a reality in the 1980s or sooner.

Japan has initiated another expansion program in South Korea, since 1965, after the Japan-Korea Treaty. Not only economic expansion, but military encroachment on Korea have been evident. The notorious Mitsuya or the Three Arrows Plan is one such example. It is designed to (1) occupy South Korea; (2) invade North Korea; and (3) suppress any revolution within Japan. This is a plan advocated by an extreme right wing group within the controlling political party in Japan, the Liberal Democrats. Korea is once again the first major target of Japanese militarism just as it was at the end of the last century.

Conditions in Asia, however, are very different today and it is unlikely that Japanese military power will be allowed to oppress the Koreans and other small nations as savagely as they did in the 1930s and the 1940s. Nevertheless, it is alarming to watch the growth of Japanese militarism, which will ultimately be a threat to peace.

The purpose of this book is to inform the American public that Japanese militarism is once again threatening our national interest.

1 Background

On November 25, 1970, Yukio Mishima made headlines by his ritual suicide conducted in traditional Samurai style in front of Masuda, the commanding officer of the eastern section of the Japanese Self-Defense Force in Tokyo.

Mishima was a brilliant forty-five-year-old Japanese novelist and poet, who had written more than fifty volumes by the age of thirty. These included *Confessions of a Mask, The Sounds of Waves, Five Modern Nō Plays, The Temple of the Golden Pavilion,* and more recently, *Decay of the Angel,* part of *The Sea of Fertility* tetralogy. All of these have been translated into English. Mishima felt that American culture and values had influenced Japan much too greatly and had made mock of Japanese tradition. *The Temple of the Golden Pavilion,* which symbolizes modern Japan, sold over 300,000 copies in Japan. The hero, Mizoguchi, said, "I hate myself, my evil, ugly, stammering self." To Mishima, modern Japan is evil and ugly because pointless anti-Japanese elements dominate it.

Mishima demanded that the Japanese National Self-Defense Force take over the government and return to the spirit of the 1930s when the Kwantung Army of Japan initiated the historically infamous Manchurian Incident in September 1931. The Self-Defense Force was first organized during the Allied occupation for the purpose of policing internal affairs. The title is somewhat misleading today in view of the group's size and scope. Mishima also referred to the radical young army officers who took over the city of Tokyo for three days in February of 1936.[1] Such extreme actions characterized the aggressively militaristic spirit of the 1930s that he idealized.

On that fateful November day in 1970, the author and Samurai Mishima urged 2000 of his personal followers as well as the members of the Japanese National Self-Defense Force to overthrow the existing government. He spoke for ten minutes from a balcony, then he committed ritual suicide. Mishima, by his act, wanted to demonstrate to the people how serious he was about the decay of Japanese culture. In his last speech he said that only the National Self-Defense Force possessed the real soul of Japan.

The present Japanese constitution denies political actions by the National Self-Defense Force, a product of foreign influence resulting from the Yalta and Potsdam Conferences, prior to the end of World War II. Therefore, according to Mishima, Japan ought to change her constitution. Only through such a drastic measure could Japan recover face and prestige, and reestablish true Japanese culture, history, and tradition with the emperor as the central figure. Then, Mishima incited his audience to take radical action in the name of the emperor as had happened before in the 1930s.

The Mishima incident is not an isolated one. The revival of Japanese militarism has become increasingly apparent in the last decade, even though the American government has tried to minimize such a manifestation. Mishima openly advocated a military coup d'état, and he himself was an active member of the Self-Defense Force. "If there is any Samurai Japanese spirit among us, we can't wait any longer; we must have a military coup at once!"

Mishima's Death Mourned

Mishima's efforts have not been wasted. Prime Minister Sato commented at the Diet on the day after his death that there should be other means to change the constitution than losing a talented young writer. Mishima eventually became a kind of hero. The Japanese press commented on his deed as "an act of beauty," "a mind of patriotism," and "revival of Japanese Bushido Spirit." Also, they did not hesitate to comment on the necessity of a stronger Self-Defense Force. They did not need to emphasize that point since the government had already started strengthening the military forces with their Fourth Self-Defense Plan, initiated in 1972, that will continue until 1976. By then, Japan will not only be a major economic power, but a military power as well. In former Prime Minister Kishi's words, Japan is indeed "an economic animal," and soon to become a military one.

At Mishima's official funeral, to which many thousands of his followers, members of the Self-Defense Force, politicians, writers, and public officers came, the speakers praised Mishima as a man who inherited the noble spirit of Japanese Bushido (ancient art and code of warfare). These mourners made it clear that his death style was indeed an admirable one. Hence, the military symbolism implied in his act was praised in public. Not unexpectedly, the Japanese government has since openly supported a movement to revive the Bushido spirit. Such a movement also coincided with the expansion program of the Japanese armed forces. The estimated budget for the Fourth Self-Defense Plan (1972–1976) is three times higher than it was in preceding years. Japan plans to produce all types of military planes, tanks, helicopters, as well as other new weapons for her own use.

With such a military program, Mr. Sato, then the prime minister, said in his television address in October 1971, Japan, not the United States, must take major responsibility to keep peace and order in Asia. The statement had a familiar ring.

It has been projected that Japan will soon become the third largest military power in contrast to her world rank of seventh in 1974. Furthermore, Japan now possesses all of the ingredients necessary to produce nuclear weapons.

So why are we concerned about the revival of Japanese militarism? And why is there such a revival? How much power is held by the military-industrial complex in Japan? What role do the American government and corporations play in the revival of militarism in Japan? What did it mean when Prime

Minister Sato declared in 1973 that it was not unconstitutional to send the Japanese army to South Korea to defend Japanese interests there?

At this time, is there any reason for us to be alarmed about Japanese military expansion? Why are Premiers Chou En-lai and Kim Il-sung so alarmed about Japanese military expansion? Why aren't the United States and her allies equally alarmed?

Mishima's young hero, Mizoguchi, in *The Temple of the Golden Pavilion,* set fire to the beautiful golden temple and it burned to the ground. True, Japan rebuilt the golden temple from ashes, but is it necessary to repeat such tragedies in man's history? Mishima believed that evidently such steps were necessary to purify modern Japan, a real and not fictitious place. Mishima's heroes in *The Temple of the Golden Pavilion* are no different from his heroes in *Confessions of Mask* or *The Sound of Waves.* All of them appear at odds with their society —postwar Japan.

The difference between Mishima's heroes and the Japanese government is that the former are alienated from modern Japanese society while the latter are anxious to retain Japanese postwar economic prosperity. Both of them, of course, agree that it is necessary to preserve the traditionally conservative Japanese society. As happened during the 1930s, and considering Mishima's fervent pleas to return to the values and spirit of that time, there is once again contradiction and conflict between the military-industrially oriented ruling class and the "no more Hiroshima" oriented masses regardless of their postwar economic prosperity. The zaibatsu groups, the great, oligarchical business empires that wielded tremendous power and influence in the past, have become stronger than ever. They have concentrated more on economic growth now than in prewar days, but their political control is more absolute than ever before.

During the prewar days, the zaibatsu groups had to struggle with the military groups. For example, there have been General Ugaki's policy v. General Minami's policy in Korea, the Mitsui-oriented army policy v. the Mitsubishi-oriented navy policy, the conservative army v. the "liberal" navy, the army v. the bureaucracy, and so forth. Today, however, zaibatsu groups dominate not only economic policy but political and military policies as well. Political positions including the prime minister have been decided by the Keitanren or the Economic Association[2] in Tokyo rather than by the majority political party, the Liberal-Democratic Party.

All-Powerful Zaibatsu

The zaibatsu simply became the holding companies of the Japanese national economy as well as its political bosses. How powerful are zaibatsu groups in Japan today? They control the allocation of raw materials and essentially control the market in Southeast Asia including South Korea. The zaibatsu control all of the mining products, 50 prcent of the timber, and 40 percent of the oil in Malaysia. In the last everal years, the United States has gradually permitted Japan to provide economic leadership for the Southeast Asian and South Korean economies. Japan decided to spend and invest more than six times as much abroad during the 1970s as compared to the 1960s. Government policy has clearly indicated that Japanese economic interests would be protected at any cost. How else can we interpret the more explicit position of the Japanese government in world politics except as a revival of the Japanese militarism which characterized the 1930s? Such a revival of militarism as well as the traditional Japanese cultural values was exactly the course of action that Mishima had urged his countrymen to adopt before his suicide.

The Mishima incident was not an isolated affair. It represents a serious trend in Japan today.

When two leading Japanese steel companies, Yahada and Fuji, merged as a new giant, New Japan Steel Company, second only to U.S. Steel, news of the merger did not make headlines in the American press, but certainly did in Japan. The New Japan Steel Company, which produces more than a half of Japan's total steel production, was created with that government's blessing in spite of existing antimonopoly laws in Japan. The reason behind the merger of the two steel giants was not for the purpose of international competition, as the Japanese government explained, but simply because of the nature of capitalism. Just a strong giant of a steel company was not enough, it had to be a stronger one. New Japan Steel Company will not be content to stay behind U.S. Steel but will struggle to become the largest. This is one example of the direction in which current Japanese imperialism is moving. It is moving toward a more advanced stage of imperialism. By mergers, it is building a more solid foundation at home before it intensifies the struggle against foreign competitors in the international marketplace. At this point, it is very difficult to distinguish whether political power influences economic decisions or vice versa. It will, however, become clearer when the economic powers become more demanding, as in the case of the steel merger. When economic competition is intensified, greater political demands will also become apparent.

A great deal has transpired since the first antimonopoly zaibatsu law instigated by the Allied Occupation Forces in November, 1945, to the merger of two steel giants in 1971. Yet as early as 1949, General Douglas MacArthur dominated the American military government in Tokyo and revised its original policy of the anti-zaibatsu regulation in order to strengthen the Japanese capitalistic system. The trouble had started early. It was not a matter of choosing between the welfare of the people and the maintenance of the capitalistic structure in Japan, it was an issue of how to encourage the recovery of Japan's economy. Actually, it took the Korean war to do the trick. The zaibatsu-centered, monopolistic Japanese economy was in the saddle in 1953 when the second revision of the antimonopoly regulation took place. The Japanese zaibatsu monopoly really never died even after Japan lost the war to the Allied Powers. The zaibatsu system was weakened only temporarily by the defeat of Japan, but thanks to American aid and encouragement, it is more consolidated today than ever before.

Should there be any concern about the revival of Japanese imperialism? What difference would it make to peace-loving Asians and Americans? The difference, in this writer's opinion, is the choice of freedom or slavery. The Asians are well aware of what it means to submit to Japanese domination.

My primary purpose in this book is to reveal the danger of Japanese militarism and imperialism at this time in order to preserve peace in Asia and in the rest of the world. Today, practically everyone is against imperialism. People no longer accept conquest as a natural extension of politico-economic concerns. Yet imperialism remains the primary concern of the twentieth century.

Modern imperialism differs from nineteenth-century ones in that it places its focus on economic interest in former colonies and the semi-colonial countries rather than on territorial expansion. Japan, for instance, is already in the midst of dominating the economic situation of South Korea and the Southeast Asian countries.

Notes

1. The incident is known as 2.26 military incident. The rebellious army group returned to their barracks only after the Emperor begged them to do so via radio appeal. They would normally have been punished by military court martial, but the incident was quietly settled without too much publicity.

2. Keitanren or the Association of the Business Groups is the most powerful single association and influences Japan's postwar politico-economic policy.

2 Birth of a Military Nation-State

Militarism has been a characteristic feature of Japan and has been even more prominent during the nineteenth and twentieth centuries. The leaders of the Meiji Restoration (1868 –1912) produced a progressive and modern Japan, but the very nature and flavor of feudalism remained largely untouched in much of Japanese society. The existence of a military elite—the Samurai—was a major obstacle in changing from a feudal to a modern society.

The military class had controlled the Japanese government since the twelfth century and had no obvious intention of relinquishing that power even during the Meiji Restoration. The Meiji Restoration is known as the beginning of modern Japan since Emperor Meiji, grandfather of the present Emperor Hirohito, restored its sovereign power on January 3, 1868. This imperial restoration was no more than a symbolic political gesture, and the militaristic feudal system remained. The military had provided a group of leaders whom the people would follow, and the dominant military power over the civilian element in the government posed a real obstacle to the development of liberalism in Japan.

Tokugawa Establish Dynasty

It was not until 1603, when the Tokugawa clan established military control over the country, that the shogunate, or the administration of a generalissimo, ceased to change hands and internal peace was established. The Tokugawa ruled the nation for more than 260 years, and there is justification for applying to that period the name of the dynasty that actually ruled. By its conduct of foreign policy and strict regulation of public and private life, the Tokugawa dynasty left so deep an imprint on the people and the country that the components of earlier culture were able to perpetuate themselves only in the particular forms which the Tokugawa period allowed. During this important era of Japanese history, the natural isolation of the country was deliberately cultivated to a point where Japan was completely cut off from the outside world. The 260 years of peace were a period of undisturbed development, such as was never enjoyed by any Western culture. Farmlands were transformed and yielded riches to the powerful. In broad bourgeois circles, arts and crafts reached a high stage of development. Eventually, the economic growth hastened the downfall of the Tokugawa regime. This was due primarily to the fact that although times were rapidly changing, the Tokugawa refused to change their admonitions concerning proper social conduct and their feudalistic economic outlook. The long-time ruling house began to lose more and more control, especially over powerful feudal lords. "Out of a national revenue of twenty-eight or twenty-nine million 'koku' the representatives of supreme power, the Tokugawa shogun and the court, allocated to themselves only about eight million koku, while by far the larger part of the revenue remained in the hands of great feudal vassals."[1]

Also, the attempts of the shogunate to revive the stricken economy in the 1830s were futile and generally lacking in any realistic concepts of how to deal with the situation. "They tried, of course, the old policy of government by exhortation, and issued edicts on thrift at intervals from the seventeenth to the nineteenth century, but it was idle to prescribe saving to those who had no money to spare."[2] The effect of a money economy upon the social and political institutions of Japan caused a slow but irresistible revolution, culminating in the breakdown of feudal government and resumption of intercourse with foreign countries after more than two hundred years of seclusion.

The guild system had developed with official sanction by the end of the seventeenth century. As a whole, the merchants were well-protected from arbitrary confiscation and heavy taxation although they were controlled in order to extract fees, and were held down socially by the ruling class with their Confucian contempt for commerce. This did not prevent the development of power in the merchant class. As a matter of fact, a number of great merchant houses including the house of Mitsui developed during these years. The Mitsui became official banker to the Tokugawa shogun in 1691.

The indebtedness of the top ruling class to the socially lowest class of merchants obviously undermined the entire Tokugawa feudal society. The despised merchant class had increasingly influenced the economic and cultural patterns and the bureaucrats who were transformed Samurai suffered more than any others.

The drastic effects caused by a change from a barter to a money economy are reflected in the estimate that by 1850 more than 90 percent of all the property of the Daimyo, or feudal lords, and Samurai had been mortgaged to the merchant-financier class. With the misery of the peasants and the failure to tax the wealth of the townspeople proportionately, meant that Tokugawa Japan was bankrupt.

Soon the entire system of feudalism was collapsing. Until Commodore Perry forced open the doors of Japan, the Tokugawa rulers had failed completely to comprehend the economic collapse that was occurring.

The policy of isolating Japan from all foreign contacts had prevented alliances and consequent influx of foreign ideas. For well over two centuries, the shogunate had maintained the fiction that the emperor ruled and the shogun carried out his wishes, but this was recognized by all as a mere political device. Opposition to Tokugawa rule had been constantly growing during this period, but it was not until the nineteenth century that there emerged several ideological lines of attack that could be used to challenge the shoguns' position.

During the peaceful period of Tokugawa, actually, there

was no need for a military profession, but on the other hand, there was no way to relinquish a class that was as large as two million out of a total of some thirty million in population. The Samurai were a parasitic class and unproductive. They were, however, useful to the feudal rulers. The rest of the people were told what to do and what was to be expected of them. They were told that the ruler was a superior person who would always provide good government. This notion was based on the Confucian ideas of Chinese society where the people were expected to obey the laws and follow their leaders willingly and blindly. The emphasis was on the state rather than on the citizens.

Loyalty was an ancient Bushido concept. The intense loyalty which Bushido emphasized as the cardinal virtue was an instrument of that policy. The feudal ethical principles of unquestioning loyalty to one's master, strict fulfillment of one's responsibility, and maintaining one's honor became a modern military code of ethics. This is the spirit of Bushido or the Way of the Warrior. The Bushido spirit not only became the military code of ethics but became a general ethical practice in Japan.

The development of militarism was associated closely with the decentralization of power, the rise of feudalism, and the expansion of Japanese territory.

Since the central government was unable to protect them, the feudal lords, landlords, and officials needed to defend themselves, particularly during the wars against the Ainu people, one of the early settlers in Japan. Accordingly, private armies of varying sizes came into existence. Thus, new families gradually came to the forefront with wealth and power based on land, and strengthened by their armed retainers, the Samurai.

The clan and family tradition, so strong in Japan from the earliest times, persisted and took on new forms adapted to the needs of the times.

The most prominent of these early families supplied the Daimyo, or the great names. Their armed retainers became the Samurai, "those who serve," a warrior caste. The military class exalted as virtues complete loyalty to the clan and the lord, physical courage, and contempt of death. The sword became its badge and symbol. The sword became an all-important symbol and its manufacture began to gain attention as a distinct art form.

From these various ideas, the Meiji Restoration leaders chose to emphasize the theory that in ancient times the imperial institution had enjoyed great power and prestige and that the shogun was an usurper who had taken all real authority away from the emperor.

Downfall of Tokugawa

The end of Tokugawa shogunate seemed only a matter of time, and its downfall was hastened by Western pressures. The Russians were the first to exert pressure on Japan during the eighteenth century, and the British, too, were beginning to appear in Japanese waters. English vessels visited Hokkaido in 1797 and Nagasaki in 1808. The United States was, however, the first nation to open Japan through the efforts of Commodore Matthew C. Perry. The Treaty of Kanagawa between the two nations was signed on March 31, 1854. Japan was politically backward and economically feudalistic. She was no match for the Western powers. The treaty signalled the end of the dynasty for the Tokugawa shogun. The shogunate was forced to recognize the imperial court as the ultimate political authority.

The imperial court, at this time, was not able to fill the political vacuum created by Tokugawa shogun. Besides, the new Emperor Mutsuhito, or Meiji, was only a child of fourteen when Emperor Komei died in 1867. Nevertheless, Meiji became the symbol of modern Japan. Meantime, a handful of young Samurai elites from Choshu, Satsuma, Hizen, and Tosa in western Japan seized the opportunity for political control in the imperial court of Kyoto.

The new leaders—Kido, Okubo, Saigo, Ito—were all young men of Samurai origin and they realized that Japan was no match for Western military and industrial power. They were determined to learn from the West. It was clear to them that Japan had to have a much more centralized and modernized government that had to institute major economic and social reforms.

The merchants contributed financially to the revolution and exerted their influence together with the Samurai elite upon governmental affairs in modernizing Japan. This was a revolutionary attempt and was to have profound influence on the future of Japan.

The attitude of the leaders of the Meiji Restoration was shown very clearly by the manner in which they handled the Tokugawa after their final defeat. The fiefdoms that had been seized were administered directly as property that belonged to the central government. The movements which ushered in the era of Meiji were called by its initiators Fukko or The Return to Antiquity. But the leaders obviously had something else in mind other than the restoration of feudalism under the emperor and a return to the good old days. They were neither lacking in a sense of direction nor in the skills of the professional revolutionary. The breakdown of feudalism was followed in the next few years by actions that created and perfected a thoroughly centralized government. In place of the old feudal army, made up of contingents furnished by individual fiefs and recruited exclusively from the Samurai, a national army was substituted, drawn from all ranks of society. The result of this national conscription was to become evident in the later years.

Meiji Reform

To no class was now reserved the privilege of defending the state; the opportunity for doing so was not only offered, but demanded by a system of compulsory military training. Closely related to this was the removal of many of the old social distinctions. The difference between the civil or court nobility and the military class was abolished. The new aristocracy subsequently created was neither civil nor military, but national.[3] This brilliant opportunism of the Meiji leaders stemmed probably from their sense of dedication to Japan, their personal ambitions, as well as their factional interests. Unlike their predecessors, they were willing to adapt to the changing times. It was apparent to them that a new military system could not be maintained without a new political and economic system. They were willing to acquire from the West much of the knowledge they needed for their own specific purpose of building up the national strength of Japan. They were also quick to add new, and modernize old, systems. By and large they chose well, selecting what they wanted with the trained eyes of men who had not only seized but were creating new power. The oligarchy released enormous social energies by changing the relationship between the classes in their attempt to set up a new institutional pattern. A new constitution was established in 1889. The Restoration leaders were seeking more efficient ways to gain political power.

Emperor Deemed Sacred

The constitution was drafted by a committee attached to the Ministry of Imperial Household which was very influencial in the workings of the new government. The drafting took place behind locked doors without public discussion or contact with public opinion. It, in effect, embodied traditional Japanese political principles under the cloak of representative institutions. Since the structure of the state was considered eternal, the constitution contained no provisions for amendment by the legislative branches. The new instrument fully protected the ancient prerogatives of the throne and those who represented it. Article One declared, "The Empire of Japan shall be reigned over and governed by a line of Emperors unbroken for ages eternal." Article Three proclaimed, "The Emperor is sacred and inviolable," while the succeeding article declared, "The Emperor is the head of the empire, combining in himself the rights of sovereignty, and exercises them according to the provisions of the present constitution." Thus, the competence of the crown was unlimited.

On the one hand, the emperor was above criticism; on the other, the legislative and executive powers culminated in him and nothing could be decided without his consent or that of his personal advisors. The parliament was given little power and in any conflict its defeat was a foregone conclusion. Crown and governmental influence was further reinforced by a series of institutions such as the genro or elder system. The end result was that the position of the monarch was the same as it would have been without the parliament; vital decisions were rendered on his authority, and were affected only by the inner communications he maintained. Therefore, while in effect, the constitution was merely a concession to popular government with the oligarchy retaining practically all powers; it illustrated the political agility of the revolutionaries. They were as much concerned with political conservatism as with economic innovation.

The Constitution of 1889 was the public and written description of the manner in which the oligarchy proposed to rule Japan. Still more important was the question of why it was able to remain in control for so long and with such effectiveness. This can best be answered in the emperor worship concept. The intellectual preparation for the Restoration had centered around the revival of the ancient glories of Japan and of the emperor institution. It was this institution that was to be a symbol of unity to a clannish and warring people. Loyalty was created when the territorial lords were separated from their lands and their peasants. The vacuum was filled with the much larger emperor concept.

Shinto Revived by Meiji

The emperor worship idea was actually derived from Shintoism. Shinto, to begin with, is not a Japanese term for the religion. It is the Chinese equivalent of what the Japanese call *Kami no michi,* meaning "the way of the gods," and had come into popular usage. Shintoism was a remnant of primitive nature worship long prevailing among tribes on the islands of Japan, subsequently developed and shaped according to the degree of civilization attained. In effect, Shinto as a religion was an unorganized worship of spirits. It was rooted in the instinctive feeling of being in communion with all living forces of the world and showed its vitality in a communal cult. For Shinto worship was often connected with local legends and communal customs, and the deities thus worshipped were mostly considered to be ancestral or tutelary spirits of the universal origin of the common people. Shinto must also be considered as being preeminently the religion of an agrarian people. The frequent manifestation of the spirits of plants and corn, the intimate relationship existing between the people and the universal deities, the close ties binding the divinities with things of nature, all tended to indicate the life of an agricultural people settled down in close communities. And when it had been more or less organized in the course of several centuries to about the eighth, emphasis was laid on the supremacy of the Sun-Goddess, Amaterasu-O-mikami, ancestress of all Japanese people, while the emperor, a direct descendant of the Sun-Goddess, was the father of his people. Thus the so-called divinity of the Japanese imperial line was established. Both gods and nature deities were often symbolized by such objects as mirrors, swords, and so forth. Nature worship came to be called Shinto or the "way of gods" in order to distinguish it from Buddhism.

Shintoism, however, was not a popular religion in Japan. The gradual introduction of Chinese culture, dating from about the third century of the Christian era, and that of Buddhism in the sixth century, were concurrent with a vigorous social growth in Japan. Buddhism, the new religion, imported many arts and sciences, letters and philosophy, all working as instruments of its propagation, and through the astounding progress of its missionary work, the country came under the influence of Buddhism during the seventh century.

Compared to a great religion like Buddhism, the Shintoistic concept was a meager and shallow one. Its entire content could be summed up in the phrase, "Fear the gods and obey the emperor," and the notion that the land, its people, and especially the ruler, were divine. But in considering the rivalry between Buddhism and Shintoism, it must be remembered that Buddhism was practiced principally by the upper classes. Unorganized Shintoism, which has been shown to be little more than the expression of traditional Japanese ways of thinking about life, did not come into conflict with Buddhist doctrine, and its beliefs persisted with little change. They did not disappear into Buddhist theology. The concept of the divine right of the emperor was too valuable for the rulers to put aside. This theory also eventually aided in the transformation of the functions of the emperor. He was surrounded with mysterious splendor, and removed, as much as a god, from his people. Therefore, the control of mundane affairs more and more slipped from his hands into the grasp of men who had to do with the realities of the empire and its people. Divinity and exaltation became separated from power and rule. Thus, the era of the shoguns was established, a period in which the military lords ruled, although the emperor was the official government head.

While the Japanese leaders of the Meiji Restoration had shown their determination to learn from each Western country that in which it particularly excelled, they realized that this was not the whole solution to their needs. With its predominant strength, the new government naturally paid great attention to the creation of a strong army and navy along Western lines. However, the leaders knew that to be truly strong, the new army and navy needed behind them an efficient and stable political system, a physically strong and technically competent people, and a sound and industrially advanced economy. Thus, while building up the army and navy, they by no means neglected the other requisites for national strength. The traditional loyalty of the people was there; now the transformation must be made in the minds of the people to rest on the new government. The methods effecting the transformation of loyalty centered principally around building up the emperor idea. This was deliberately done by the Meiji Restoration leaders. The emperor's powers had been defined by the constitution. No one could criticize the constitution since no one was permitted to criticize the emperor. Since the emperor, pictured as heaven-descended, divine, sacred, all-wise, and virtuous, was set apart from the nation, all people were forbidden to make him even a topic of discussion, much less of a derogatory comment.

As the sovereign rights of the state were transmitted to the emperor, it was logical that the ministers should be responsible to the emperor rather than to the people. The oligarchy could hardly have secured its position more thoroughly than it did by monopolizing access to absolute authority. But defining the emperor's position was not enough. For it to be widely accepted, there had to be an emotional basis for the necessary reverence and obedience. The oligarchy attempted to do this by making the emperor the central figure in a revived and officially sponsored Shinto religion.

Shinto and Nationalism

The revival of Shintoism was easy, because it merely represented a continuation of traditional religious beliefs and practices. To myths concerning the origin of Japan and its ruling houses were added worship of the nation's heroes and its imperial ancestors. As such, it was identified closely with patriotism and gave a religious tinge to the ensuing nationalistic aspect. State Shintoism was placed under a government department different from that of other religions. "Thus there was a re-establishment of the theocratic idea as embodied in the institution of the Jingi-Kan, or National Cult Department."[4] It emphasized the building of shrines and supported a large priesthood. State Shinto insisted that the reigning emperor and his ancestors were divine. Throughout the entire cult, the superiority of the Japanese as a race, their divine mission in the world, and their supreme devotion to the emperor were stressed. Japan was pictured as an invincible nation. To reach the young and begin their indoctrination early, Shinto shrines were placed in every school. Shinto rituals were made a fundamental part of the training of every school child. By an imperial edict of 1890, Japanese youth were taught that the imperial throne was as ancient as the very origins of heaven and earth. Portraits of the emperor were also provided for each school. Any failure to display appropriate respect for the imperial institution or any attempt to question the factual basis of Japanese mythology indicated a lack of knowledge of the duties and place of the person as a fortunate subject of the divine emperor. While it is true that the history was ridiculously inaccurate, still it served its purposes well. "Ancient and impressive national beginnings, dim legends of a glorious decline from the gods, became registered in the national conscience through the purely political device of falsified historical writings."[5] The state financially supported this intensely nationalistic endeavor, and it was money well spent. Thus the Meiji Restoration was developing an instrument of state capable of producing the blind loyalty and devotion Japan's leaders required. To the reformers, education meant not the development of young minds for participation in a fuller life, but rather the training of a technically competent citizenry to help build a strong state. Education, therefore, was essentially designed as a tool of government training of obedient and reliable subjects who would serve well in the machinery of the modern state. The schools became increasingly a medium for teaching the people what to think rather than how to think. Thus, Japan pioneered the concept of utilizing the educational system for political indoctrination. In classrooms and in army barracks, young Japanese men were taught to glorify Japan's military traditions. They came to believe that death on the battlefield for the sake of the emperor was the most glorious fate of man, and they also believed in the unique virtues of a vaguely defined national system and an even more vague Japanese spirit. Together, the government and army succeeded in just a few decades in creating in the average Japanese the fanatical nationalism already characteristic of the upper classes, and an even more fanatical devotion to the emperor, cultivated by historians and the Shinto creed, and fostered by the oligarchy around the throne. Unlimited readiness to prove veneration for the emperor was in evidence. Viscount Oura, minister of commerce in 1908, declared, "The majesty of our imperial house towers above everything else in the world, and we take it for granted that it is as perdurable as heaven and earth. If it is contended that our country needs a religious faith then, in my opinion, we must adopt the religion of imperialism, in other words, the worship of the emperor."[6] Japanese political and military indoctrination was indeed thorough and spectacularly successful.

Religious Patriotism

As previously mentioned, Shintoism had long been in the background prior to the restoration and had been influenced by Buddhism. Still it had remained all the while very much alive in the minds of most of the people, as evidenced by the short time its revival took. However, even after being put into the place of honor, it soon became obvious that as a systematized religion, Shintoism could not maintain itself. This was of no importance whatsoever, for its value did not lie in that sense of religion. Differentiation must be made between Shinto as a formal religion (if it ever was thought of as such), and as a creed or way of life. It is in the latter sense that the true value was found and in that concept rather than in ritualized ceremonies. "The legends, cosmology, and pseudo-history are not the religion, and its power is not in dogmas nor in forms of worship; it is a spirit, the spirit of ancient Japan, Yamato-damashi."[7] Therefore, the essential element in Shintoism was the religious patriotism it could instill in the people. From this, the Restoration leaders were able to mold an extraordinary instrument for creating a mass loyalty to the imperial institution and to the person of the emperor. This was the pliability of the Shinto creed. There is nothing inherently impossible, or even improbable, in the idea of the Japanese declaring themselves as Shintoists. It was not at all impossible to think as Shintoists and believe that a different regime could be established in Japan, so long as that regime preserved the spirit of Yamato-damashi or Japanese soul, and retained the deification of the imperial person and position. The basic elements of old Japan still existed; the new government had only to appeal to them. Among these basic elements may also be included the family and ancestor cult, but above all, it was the concept of a deified and inviolable emperor that had been taught by the ancient Shinto.

Thus, the Japanese were taught to identify themselves as citizens in the abstract—subject to authority embodied in the magistrate's office, but having a direct personal relationship with a divine emperor.

Notably, this personal loyalty was still being appealed to just as it had been under the feudal system. Obligation to the emperor overshadowed all others, and may even have been viewed as the source of all other duties—a supreme ethical commandment. No words, however extravagant, would seem adequate to a Japanese patriot to describe his veneration for the emperor. True loyalty was now the source of all virtue in the state. It was not so much an obligation toward the divine imperial house as it was a privilege. The individual's development was met only in terms of the needs of the state.

The imagination and vision of the Meiji leaders cannot be underestimated. Their idea of raising the person of the emperor to a sacred and inviolable status, of merging the imperial household into the very bloodstream of Japanese history and tradition, of making an object of national worship out of something so little known and so recently insignificant, was quite possibly the only solution bold and dramatic enough to meet a situation in which an old order was dying and the people were open to foreign ideologies. The emperor idea was the only thing big enough to fill the need. While it exploited existing Japanese values of loyalty and obligation, it was simple enough for everyone to understand, it could be related to every aspect of life and daily living, and it was easily identified and not easily confused with anything else in the world. But again, most importantly it proposed an idea that the people were traditionally adapted to accept because of their cultural background and Shinto way of life.

As repeatedly suggested, the effects of the Meiji Restoration and the successes of the oligarchy could not help but result in strong nationalistic tendencies. Since the emperor and the state were considered to be one and the same thing, and the emperor could be worshipped as the theoretical head of the state, Japanese nationalism easily evolved and grew in a form that was unusual at the time. "The spirit of nationalism which had been growing, even if feebly, under the Tokugawa regime, and which had been roused into sudden, vigorous life by renewed contact with the nations of the West, had expressed itself inwardly in a centralization and complete reorganization of the state."[8] There was an increased interest in imperialism, a desire to expand, almost from the date of its birth. A demand for equality with Western powers was evident everywhere, arising from the growing spirit of national pride that would not put up with discrimination from any. It is difficult to find the correct conceptual terms to express this fanatical devotion to the country stemming from the relation established between the dynasty and the people.

Even the Russian type of autocracy does not offer an exact parallel. In Russia, the czar was the absolute ruler, above criticism and above approbation. He ruled by divine grace, but in his own person the czar was not divine, nor of divine origin. However elevated, he was human, since he belonged to the circle of those who professed Christianity. But the Japanese dynasty, like the Japanese people, was isolated on a small island. Descended from heaven, with the blood of the gods in its veins, the imperial family was *sui generis.*

Japan Resents Western Powers

Unfortunately, in all the dealings of Westerners with the Japanese during the first years of the Meiji era, there was an assumption of superiority, a tendency to treat Japanese in a condescending and patronizing way which was very galling to the proud and sensitive people. Even at this early stage, many avid Japanese nationalists advocated settling the matter by warfare. But, fortunately, for them, their leaders were wise enough to build up the country's strength first so that they might demand respect as their proven right. Still many harbored deep resentment at being treated as inferiors. "We will learn all you can teach and then—we will fight you,"[9] was the frank statement of many Japanese patriots of the day. Later, after the government began to become much stronger and the people more conscious of the ways of the progressive West, the attitude of hostility was superseded by a strong desire to win recognition. After conforming greatly to Western standards both in social and economic aspects, the Japanese felt that they had the right to new treaties and concessions that would admit them into the circle of civilized nations. When diplomatic endeavors toward this objective failed, a wave of indignant protest spread throughout Japan. The antiforeign sentiment again came to the fore. There were two main points of issue at this time that were causing the friction between Japan and the treaty powers. One was the system of extraterritoriality and the other was the conventional tariff. "The former was introduced in the Russian treaty of 1855, repeated in the Dutch and American treaties of 1856 and 1857, and clearly defined in the commercial treaties of 1858, in regard to civil as well as criminal cases."[10] "The latter was found in the four-power convention of 1866 which took the place of the tariff regulations in the 1858 treaties and subsequent amendments."[11]

Extraterritoriality

The Japanese people had taken up the agitation, and from the early 1880s tariff autonomy and the abolition of extraterritoriality were vigorously demanded both from the press and public platform. Halfway measures were not welcome. Therefore, the Japanese refused a concession offered by the powers in 1886 whereby the jurisdiction of their courts would extend to foreigners, provided that they were all cases in which foreign judges had been appointed. The Japanese obviously wanted equality, not minor concessions. Extraterritoriality meant exemption from the jurisdictional application of local law. The right exercised by most Western governments throughout Asia was to have their nationals tried by their courts rather than by native laws. President Franklin D. Roosevelt denounced such practice in China during the war against Japan in 1943.

Since diplomacy and some degree of conformity did not seem to bring Japan much closer to her goal of equality with Western nations, it began to appear that other more forceful measures more to the liking of Japanese nature would have to be taken. This involved the adoption of imperialistic policies and was to prove much more successful in attaining the desired goals. In fact, the Meiji reformers, who began in 1868 to make Japan into a modern nation—able to hold its own on terms of equality with the Western powers—were to see their ambitions realized within their own lifetimes. With the assistance of a powerful army and navy, an efficient government, a patriotic citizenry, and a vigorous industry and commerce, Japan made herself into a world military power within a few decades and won recognition of equality from occidentals, who had tended to look upon all Asian peoples as primarily barbarians and outside the elite grouping of civilized nations. This included the Chinese prior to opening her door to the West in the nineteenth century. The Chinese regarded all nations who did not accept her civilization as barbaric.

"Japanese leaders, with their Samurai backgrounds, enthusiastically embraced the imperialism of Europe and soon outstripped the Western imperialists in their determination to win colonies."[12] They saw that poor and small Japan needed more natural resources to become a first-class world power, and they believed that control of adjacent territories would yield many of these sources and strengthen the defenses of Japan. Political decay and military weakness in China and Korea made these lands ripe for foreign aggression and the Japanese leaders eagerly joined Europeans in the game of winning territories and economic privileges therefrom. Besides protecting her vested rights in China, Japan used the justification that she was protecting her subjects from foreign aggressors. "In other words, to free Japanese nationals from persecution and extortion and maintain for them all rights in China to which nationals of other powers are entitled."[13]

By 1872, the Japanese had forced China to pay an indemnity as compensation for Japanese sailors who had been killed by the inhabitants of Formosa, China's island dependency. For the Japanese, this was a successful testing of their military power and growing influence in Asia. Two years later by a show of naval might, the Japanese forced King Kojong of Korea to open his land to foreign intercourse and to sign a treaty granting to Japan the special privileges usually demanded by European powers only from Asiatic states.[14] By 1894, Japan felt strong enough for a real test of strength. In that year she precipitated a war with China over the control of Korea. Japan easily seized Korea, destroyed the Chinese naval forces put against her, overran southern Manchuria, and even succeeded in capturing the port of Wei-hai-wei in China proper. By the ensuing peace treaty, China was forced to pay a large indemnity to Japan; recognize the independence of Korea; and cede to Japan the island of Formosa, the Pescadores Islands, and the Liaotung Peninsula. The dwarf had worsted the giant, and had demonstrated that it was a factor to be reckoned with in the Far East. Indeed, Japan had demonstrated that she had become a modern military power, and had made a successful step in building an empire.

The reasons for extraterritoriality were also fast disappearing and Western powers could not long continue to maintain it. In 1888, Mexico had signed a treaty granting to Japan judicial autonomy, and the United States had long been willing to take similar steps as soon as the leading European nations would agree to follow suit. Finally, impressed by the rapid and efficient reorganization of Japanese political institutions in outward conformity with Western patterns, the British in 1894 agreed to surrender their right to extraterritoriality. Other Western powers followed the British example, and in 1899 Japan became the first Asiatic to free itself of extraterritoriality. The Western nations also began to relinquish the treaty rights under which they had restricted Japanese tariffs since the late days of the Tokugawa. Thus, tariff autonomy was partially restored in 1899, although it did not completely go into effect until more than a decade later (1911).

Thus we have seen that Japan soon learned that her acceptance could be effected best through her displays of military power. This was to have a great effect on later actions and thinking, and perhaps explains the following statement: " In November, 1914, Premier Marquis Okuma publicly declared, 'Those who are superior will govern those who are inferior. I believe that within two or three centuries the world will have a few governing countries and others will be governed by them and will pay homage to their might. We should, from now on, prepare ourselves to become a governing nation.' "[15] Apparently, Japan had indeed learned her lesson well.

The various trials and imperialistic ambitions previously mentioned served merely to cause an undeniable strengthening of religio-nationalistic tendencies in Japan. From our inquiry into the Japanese way of life and thinking, this is rather a logical conclusion. Struggles for power increased the emphasis laid on Shinto, regardless of the fact that its identification with the ancestor cult and its lack of dogmatic fiber made it irrelevent to so many of the complicated moral problems and deeper religious needs of changing times. It was the very essence of the empire.

The West never truly gained this sense of a close connection between nation, state, and religion; this perception of a mystical force which from its union with the world feeds the currents of nationality. Therefore, the Westerner is probably incapable of visualizing the potentiality of the Shinto faith, or of realizing how light is the hold of an involved body of Christianity in comparison. But in Japan we have seen how the religious attitude toward the state developed into a transcendentally exalted idea of the nation as it was embodied in the imperial office. This was its power, and quite a power it proved to be. In Europe, it was not until after the breakdown of the idea of democratic legitimacy and the eclipse of humanitarian conceptions that the new abstract power state came into existence and under the form of fascism draped itself with a peculiar covering of the chosen, dynamic nation. But in Japan this same symbol of the chosen, dynamic nation evolved without difficulty out of ancient Shinto teachings, manifested itself through the imperial idea, and retained all of its feudal values. Thus, the new Japan after the restoration inherited the whole treasure of this tradition.

Japan as Nation-State

Therefore, from the moment of her entry into modern history, Japan had the form of a fully developed national state. The deification of the imperial idea, the hypersensitivity of national feeling, the warning example set by the helplessness of

China, at an early date popularized in Japan an aggressive policy which the large portion of the population always viewed as just and even as partly defensive. Accordingly, the government was repeatedly pushed onward as soon as it showed signs of compromising with the status quo. The army, of course, was the most obvious standard bearer of such an aggressive policy, but it found support in a widespread feeling of the nation's people.

The combinations of emotions with the elements of remotest antiquity as found in the Shinto convictions explain the secret of the subsequent political success and strong nationalistic temperament. Nationalism, like the spirit of Shinto, called into play not only the will, but the intellect, the imagination, and the emotions. The intellect constructs a speculative mythology or, perhaps, a theology of nationalism. The imagination fabricates an unseen world around the eternal past and everlasting future of one's nationality. Emotions arouse a joy and ecstasy in the contemplation of the national god who is all-good and all-protecting, a longing for his favors, a thankfulness for his benefits, and a feeling of awe and reverence at the immensity of his power and wisdom. Its chief rites are public rituals performed in the name and for the salvation of the whole society. Thus, it is easy to see why the ancient Shinto fostered the growth of this phenomenon and, in a sense, became almost wholly integrated into it as a concept. The effect upon the nation of Japan is almost immeasurable. Japanese patriots were content to accept, under legal conditions of freedom, the official servitude of feudal days. They were satisfied to give their talent, their strength, their utmost effort, even their lives, for the simple privilege of obeying a government that expected all sacrifices in the feudal spirit, as a national duty. Truly this was nationalism. Militarism and nationalism in Japan were thus inseparable. The more militaristic and more nationalistic one became, the more patriotic he was in the eyes of the Japanese public. A military nation was born, and she became a major menace to peace in Asia.

Notes

1. Karl A. Wittfogel, *Oriental Depotism* (New Haven, Conn.: Yale University Press, 1957), p. 200.

2. G. B. Sansom, *Japan: A Short Cultural History* (New York: Appleton-Century, 1943), p. 521.

3. Kenneth Scott Latourette, *The Development of Japan* (New York: Macmillan, 1938), p. 123.

4. Masaharu Anesaki, *History of Japanese Religion* (London: Macmillan, 1930), p. 334.

5. Ernest T. Nash, "Japan's Schizophrenia," *Asia Magazine, XLII,* 9 (March 1942), p. 527.

6. Emil Lederer and Emy Lederer-Seidler, *Japan in Transition* (New Haven, Conn.: Yale University Press, 1938), p. 150.

7. George William Knox, *The Development of Religion in Japan* (New York: Putnam, 1907), p. 77.

8. Latourette, *The Development of Japan,* p. 149.

9. Jesse Frederick Steiner, *The Japanese Invasion* (Chicago: University of Chicago Press, 1917), p. 24.

10. Payson J. Treat, *The Far East* (New York: Houghton Mifflin, 1928), p. 270.

11. Ibid.

12. Edwin O. Reischauer, *Japan: Past and Present* (New York: Houghton Mifflin, 1947), p. 134.

13. Percy Noel, *When Japan Fights* (Tokyo, Japan: Aoki, 1937), p. 10.

14. Harold W. Sunoo, *Korea: A Political History in Modern Times* (Seoul: Kunkuk University Press, 1970), Chapter 10.

15. Harley MacNair, *The Real Conflict Between China and Japan* (Chicago: University of Chicago Press, 1938), p. 107.

3 Emergence as a World Power

Japan's triumph over China in the Sino-Japanese war of 1894–1895 revealed not only how weak and corrupt the Manchu government had become, but also revealed to Western powers that Japan had become worthy of their assignation as a world power. This became more evident after the Russo-Japanese War of 1904–1905.

Japan's success in two major wars was due to her rapid adoption of Western techniques of industrialization. Japanese modernization emphasized an intense nationalism and militarism, both of which helped to place Japan in imperialistic competition. Japan was ready to begin competing openly in the Far Eastern search for colonies.

She overplayed her hand when her imperial soldiers broke into the palace and murdered Queen Min of the Korean kingdom, a leader of anti-Japanese factions, and then terrorized King Kojong in February, 1896, but such incidents were overlooked by other imperialistic powers, who had undoubtedly experienced similar events in their own colonies. Japan was eager to be on equal footing with other imperialistic powers and none other than the British Empire became the first power to recognize her as a peer through the Anglo-Japanese Alliance of 1902. Britain was willing to accept Japan as a member of the power group that early because the English nation was concerned about aggressive Russian actions in both Korea and Manchuria.

Britain Becomes Ally

The victory over China did not leave Japan with a free hand to move into Korea. When the Japanese soldiers had terrorized King Kojong, he took refuge in the Russian legation and remained there almost a year. This was a golden opportunity for the Russian government. Japan did not minimize the seriousness of the changed situation in Seoul. In the meantime, the Russians became actively engaged in timber cutting on the northern border of Korea and Ullong Island in spite of the Russo-Japanese agreement about Korea. Japan was unquestionably disturbed by Russian activities in Korea. The British Empire was ready to support Japan's role in the Far East, especially against the Czar, Nicholas II, of Russia.

In the meantime, there were two factions operating within Russia concerned about the war with Japan. A group centering about the Ministry of Finance, led by Count Witte, wished for peaceful economic penetration of the Far East, while interests associated with a group of military leaders wished for a more aggressive policy. The Czar backed the latter.

The Boer war had shown the weaknesses of the British military forces and Great Britain wanted to check the expansion of Russia into China; if Russia took Manchuria, British interests in Hong Kong, the Malay Peninsula, Burma, and even India would be threatened. As the military forces of Great Britain were not adequate to defend Manchuria, the desirability of an alliance with Japan was apparent. The British had already checked the Czar of Russia in the Crimean War.

On the other side, Japan was also drawn toward the British Isles. Great Britain had refused to join the Triple Intervention,[1] and had led the three powers to agree to the abandonment of consular jurisdiction. Close ties had been established by Britain's role as tutor in the modernization of Japan. On April 17, 1901, Prime Minister Hayashi had a meeting with Britain's Foreign Secretary Lord Lansdowne and the idea of a formal alliance was discussed and received favorably on both sides. A month later, Hayashi explained to the British that the aims of Japanese policy were the maintenance of the Open Door policy in China, preservation of China's territory and sovereignty, and the protection of Japanese interests in Korea. Although Britain was also hoping to bring Germany into an alliance at this time, by July 30, 1901, Britain's Foreign Secretary Lansdowne had given up hope on the Germans and he notified Hayashi that the time had come for a formal alliance.

On August 14, Lansdowne suggested that the Japanese prepare a draft agreement because Japan's interests were greater than Great Britain's. This greatly enhanced the feelings of the Japanese toward the alliance. On November 1, the Japanese asked the British government to submit their draft and the next ten weeks were spent working out the details. It is significant that there were no serious difficulties during the entire negotiations. Finally, the emperor sanctioned the alliance following a favorable report from the Privy Council and on January 30, 1902, the Anglo-Japanese Alliance was signed by Lord Lansdowne and Minister Hayashi. It was announced to the world on February 11, 1902.

Anglo-Japanese Alliance

The Anglo-Japanese Alliance held for the maintenance of peace and the status quo in the Far East. It agreed that the independence of Korea and China would be maintained and the opportunity for all nations to maintain a sphere of influence in these two countries would be kept open. It agreed, also, that British interests were mainly in China and Japanese interests were mainly in Korea. Neither country was to take aggressive action against Korea or China, but they could protect their own interests if necessary. Furthermore, if either power were to become engaged in a war the nonwarring power was to maintain strict neutrality. If, however, any other power joined the enemy, the other was to come to the ally's assistance, and peace could be made only by agreement of both powers. The Alliance was to continue for five years, after which it could be denounced or renewed, but if either power was engaged in a war at the end of five years, the Alliance ran until peace was established.

Although the Alliance was necessary for British interests in the Far East, the importance of the Alliance to Japan was much greater. The Alliance maintained that Japan had particular interests in Korea and it insured that in the event of war with another European power, Japan could rely on Britain's neutrality and aid. This allowed Japan a free hand in the Far East to deal with Russia. Emotionally, the Alliance was also of great importance to Japan. Japan was tremendously encouraged. Now she could claim her equal position with other imperialistic powers.

Japanese aggressive action in Korea was not just to gain extra territory and monopolize Korean markets and raw materials, but also to control her own domestic problems. Japan was having difficulty making the new constitution work. On June 2, 1894, the same day as the revolt in Korea, the Japanese Diet was dissolved for the second time in six months. There were those Japanese politicians who felt that an aggressive action leading to the unification of all factions was the only thing that would save the new constitution.

Now that Japan's position has been set forth to some extent, it is time to continue with events leading to the Sino-Japanese War. Evidently, the internal conflict within the Japanese Diet misled the Chinese leaders. Li Hung-chang, the Minister of Foreign Affairs for China, did not believe that Japan could fight. "To the Chinese the political bickering in Tokyo during the past few years was an indication of Japanese weakness. They failed to understand its alternative significance."[2] This attitude of the Chinese got them into serious trouble. Not only was their traditionally superior attitude against Japan harmful to China in view of her ill preparation for the coming war, but the Chinese were also handicapped by their lack of internal unity. The conflict among the Japanese leaders in the Diet was no more than the dispute of strategy; their common aim for the empire was the same.

China Divided, Defeated

The difference between the two countries' military strengths was as great as the gap between their governments. There were few Western-trained military officers in China. They stood out in sharp contrast to the majority of officers trained in Chinese methods. The common soldiers were very poorly equipped. "In 1894, the Japanese general staff estimated that only sixty per cent of the Chinese soldiers mobilized against Japan were armed with some kind of rifle, many carried only a pike, sword, or a spear."[3] There was little or no feeling of national unity in China then since most of the forces were provincial. The southern forces of China looked upon the war as a northern war and called it Li Hung-chang's war.

On the other hand, in Japan, the armed forces had been expanding steadily in the Meiji era. It was not until 1888, in the army

> that regiments were organized into divisions and a field force of seven divisions created, and by 1893, there were already sixteen military schools instructing 2,600 students. Generally speaking, the Japanese army was modeled on that of the British navy and engaged British instructors. By the Sino-Japanese War of 1894–1895 the navy consisted of twenty-eight vessels and twenty-four torpedo boats.[4]

The Western powers believed that neither China nor Japan was powerful enough to defeat the other and thus upset the status quo. However, Japan gained an easy victory over China. The corruption and demoralization of Li Hung-chang's forces, especially the poor supply system, was revealed by these easy victories. The Chinese army was driven out of Korea by battles in the city of Ya-shan, and then retreated to Pyong-yang where they gathered a force of 17,000 men under the command of General Tso. The Chinese resisted until the general was killed and then they fled. The defeat became a rout and left China wide open to Japan.

The Chinese finally agreed to come to terms when it looked as if there was nothing they could do to stop the Japanese from occupying Peking. The Chinese government tried to initiate several peace settlements with Japan. The first was through the Americans in Peking. This failed. The next attempt occurred when the court appointed Chang Yu-hawn and Shao Yu-lien special envoys to Japan, to inquire what terms Japan would demand to end the war. Japan refused to negotiate with the men since they did not have plenipotentiary power. Finally, in February, Li Hung-chang was appointed ambassador extraordinaire to negotiate peace with Japan. Li arrived at Shimonoseki on March 19th, and began negotiations the next day with Prime Minister Ito Hirobumi and Foreign Minister Inutsu Munemitsu. The negotiations took only a month. Li Hung-chang did his best to make the treaty less harsh on the Chinese but without much success.

For China, this war had a profound effect. The shame of being beaten by an Asian power was overwhelming. A widespread sense of panic ensued in that ancient land.

On the other hand, the victory gave the Japanese military a place of dominance in domestic affairs which became increasingly important as time went on. This ascendency was to make possible an imperialistic policy that plunged Japan into a series of wars.

Perhaps the most important event in the internal affairs of the government during this critical period was the attempt to establish a two-party government. The defeat of a bill to increase the land tax by a coalition of Liberal and Progressive parties in the Japanese Diet proved it could defeat the clan-dominated government. The Sino-Japanese War, more than anything else, helped bring about the political coalition. The Sino-Japanese War broke out on August 1, 1894, and popular enthusiasm over Japanese military successes had much to do in bringing about the cooperation between the Diet and the cabinet. This relationship suffered when the cabinet decided to return to China the Liaotung Peninsula in 1895. The confrontation between the Diet and the cabinet reached a deadlock. The situation was so tense that none of the oligarchs was willing to take the prime ministership.

On June 22, 1898, the Kenseito or Constitutional Party was created under the leadership of Okuma and Itagaki. They were assigned to reorganize the government with Okuma as prime minister and Itagaki home minister, but the new party found the heavy responsibilities burdensome because both the ministers of the army and the navy, as well as the bureaucracy as a whole, were not cooperative with the newly formed cabinet. The cabinet, organized for the first time by a political party, collapsed after only four months.[5] It was true that the coalition had been formed because of a common grievance rather than a common identity with principles.

Ito, meanwhile, had been wary of the increasing power of the Yamagata group and decided to establish a party to check the Yamagata influence and power. Yamagata was a conservative promilitary politician opposed to Ito's more Western-oriented political style. Ito chose the remnants of the Kenseito and formed a party called the Seiyukai. In many respects, the ideas of Yamagata and Ito were similar. Both were convinced of the value of the Imperial House, the Emperor, the modernization of Japan, and most of all they agreed that Japan should expand in power and influence not only in Asia, but all over the world. The reader should remember that Ito and Yamagata were both born into Samurai households and therefore both had been brought up believing in the same ideas. However, Ito had become liberalized by spending a great deal of time travelling around the world and coming into contact with foreigners, while Yamagata still retained the ideas he had learned as a child.

Ito was a statesman and was always aware of the danger of proceeding too fast, while Yamagata was a soldier and believed first and foremost in the power of the military. Thus Yamagata developed and perfected a fighting force and Ito prepared by establishing a limited parliamentary democracy so that civilians might have some control in the government. This led to differences of opinion between the two men on how, when, and where, even though their purpose of making Japan into a modern power was identical. Although the government was to fall six times between 1894 and 1904, the main ideas of expansion were held by all Japan's political-military leaders.

Yamagata used the opportunity to organize the conservative cabinet. His chief efforts were utilized in increasing the autonomy of the armed services and having the parties independent of the bureaucracy. This political pattern of strengthening military position in the government against civilian control is a consistent picture in the history of modern Japan.

Mobilization Boosted

After the Sino-Japanese War of 1894–1895, the Japanese did not demobilize their troops as most nations did, but actually increased the size of their army and navy. Because of the Triple Intervention between France, Germany, and Russia, Japan knew that she probably would have a conflict with a European power and therefore it was necessary to bring armed forces up to the level of a Western power. Japan was able to finance this expansion with the indemnity, 200 million taels of silver, she had received from the Chinese.

At the end of the war, five new divisions were created and the organization was changed so that the cavalry, artillery, and engineers were attached independently to the infantry divisions. The defense of the home Islands was greatly augmented after the war by planting mines around the harbors of Japanese cities and increasing the number of artillery batteries defending the harbors. Efforts were made to make Japan self-sufficient and therefore all the arsenals of Japan were overhauled to make any kind of ammunition the Japanese army or navy might need. The length of compulsory service in the army was also increased to twelve years—three in the active army, and then nine years in the reserves. There were also one-year volunteers who were able to extend their liability while they were in school or some other occupation. When they became twenty-eight years old, they had to join up for one year as well as pay for all their own expenses. Better rifles for the infantry and guns for the artillery batteries were secured. These were quick-firing, breech-loading guns which greatly increased the fire-power of the army. These were manufactured in Japan and were of the largest type available in 1902. By this time, the resources of Japan had become equal to the task of supplying weapons needed by the army.

Table 1

Comparative Figures of Armed Forces in Japan[6]

	Before Sino-Japanese War 1894-1895	Before Russo-Japanese War 1904-1905
Generals	36	94
Higher Officers and Officers	4235	8480
Petty Officers	8970	11,865
Trained Men	65,241	132,348
Untrained Men	185,000	425,000
Divisions	7	13

Table 1 compares the forces of Japan before the Sino-Japanese War and just before the Russo-Japanese War. It shows the great increase of the Japanese army in the years following the war with China. The significance of this increase is that Japan realized that she still had not achieved world power status and that she still must prepare her armies for the future. Even though the civilian government was opposed to such large increases in armament spending, there was little they could do because the ministers of war and navy would simply resign if they did not receive the money they needed and this would cause the government to fall.

Also, the navy was in a period of expansion as shown by the chart on page 40. At the beginning of the Sino-Japanese War, the navy was not large, but well-equipped and manned by well-trained officers and men. The admirals directing the fleets were also of the highest quality and Admiral Togo's victory over the Russians in the Russo-Japanese War proved this. The Russian Baltic fleet was all but annihilated on May 27–28, 1905, in the Sea of Japan. The help and influence of the British Navy was also of significant value, for then Britannia still ruled the waves. Again the huge indemnity received from the Chinese played an important part by paying for the expansion of the Japanese navy, also indicated on the chart below.

By 1904, the Japanese navy was ready. They were now able to confront the Russians with six battleships of 84,652 tons; eight armored cruisers of 73,982 tons; and forty-four other smaller cruisers totaling 111,470 tons. This was a sizeable increase in capital ships over the Sino-Japanese War. Although Japan occasionally had ships built outside of Japan she preferred to build them herself. It was a rule by 1900 that, if possible, every part of the ship including the hull, the armor, the guns, and the equipment had to come from Japan. Since 1903, only three ships had been built outside of Japan. They were the *Koshima,* the *Katori,* and the *Kongo,* which were built in England.

It is difficult to determine a specific period of time in the rise of Japan that was absolutely and positively necessary in Japan's rise to a world power. The thesis, however, could be developed that probably the ten-year period following the Sino-Japanese War was the most important in Japan's rise to modern power status. This viewpoint can be supported by certain turns

Table 2

Japanese Naval Forces: 1894–1904[7]

	Before Sino-Japanese War 1894-1895	Before Russo-Japanese War 1904-1905
Battleships	1	6
Armored Cruisers	4	8
Cruisers	7	20
Light Cruisers	9	9
Destroyers	0	19
Motor Torpedo boats	24	85
Others	11	....

of events in Japan. The first was the opening of Japan by Commodore Perry in 1853. This encounter with the Western world was forced upon the Japanese by the presence of American warships along with Perry. The Japanese had cut themselves off from the world in 1790 and if they had wanted to renew trade with the West they would have had to have opened their doors eventually. But since Perry had forced them open, the Japanese people had lost face and this, too, began to instill a spirit of nationalism and revenge in the back of Japanese minds. The next event was the Meiji Restoration, which gave new impetus to the beginnings of nationalism in Japan. Although unity was not established until the Satsuma Rebellion[8] was crushed in 1877, the beginning of the unity of purpose was strongly established by the Meiji Restoration.

By successful wars against China and Russia (and the Anglo-Japanese Alliance, the most important event in foreign affairs), Japan had become recognized as a world power. To maintain its status as a world power, and to fulfill imperialistic ambitions, a program of government-owned monopolies in industry was started as well as the initiation of a land tax to finance them. Later these industries were sold to the zaibatsu, a group of powerful financial cliques. The zaibatsu, notably Mitsui, Mitsubishi, Sumitomo, and Yasuda, formed great monopolies, encouraged and supported the modern military expansion in the Far East, and kept nurturing Japan as a military power in the world.

Notes

1. At the conclusion of the Sino-Japanese War, the three powers—Russia, Germany, and France—demanded that Japan return Liaotung Peninsula to China. They claimed that their action was primarily concern over peace in Asia. Japan returned it reluctantly, and began to prepare herself militarily to be mightier than ever.

2. George M. Beckman, *The Modernization of China and Japan* (New York: Harper and Row, 1962), p. 131.

3. Ibid., p. 151.

4. Sir Esler Dening, *Japan* (New York: Praeger, 1961), pp. 50–51.

5. The government was forced to resign when its minister of education said, in a lecture before the Imperial Education Association, "Suppose that you dreamed Japan had adopted a republican form of government, a Mitsui or a Mitsubishi would immediately become the presidential candidate." Because he had insinuated that the Japanese government might be a republic even hypothetically, the government had to resign. Herbert Norman, *Japan's Emergence as a Modern State* (New York: Institute of Pacific Relations, 1940), p. 192.

6. William M. McGovern, *Modern Japan* (New York: Scribner, 1920), p. 176.

7. Robert P. Porter, *Japan, The Rise of a Modern Power* (London: Oxford, 1918), pp. 319–320.

8. The Satsuma Rebellion was led by Saigo Takamori, one of the elite members of the Meiji Restoration. Saigo left the government and went into opposition. He led a large-scale rebellion numbering about 40,000 troops against the government's 60,000. The civil war continued for eight months. Saigo died in combat. The civil war was a major violence during the Meiji Restoration.

4 The Manchurian Incident

The Manchurian Incident was the most significant politico-military affair in the Far East since Japan's annexation of Korea in 1910. It heralded the beginning of World War II. Japan invaded Manchuria in September, 1931, with tacit approval of the imperialist powers led by Great Britain. No major power made any serious protest to Japan in spite of the obvious violation of Chinese sovereignty, previously guaranteed by the major powers through numerous international treaties. The *London Times* justified the action of Japan while the United States was satisfied with Secretary of State under Herbert Hoover Henry Stimson's token protest. Even the Nationalist government under Chiang Kai-shek made no serious attempt to condemn Japan's aggression. All agreed that the Japanese invasion of Manchuria could very well liquidate the growing Communist movement in Manchuria and this was considered a very good thing. There had also been serious attempts by the Russians to establish a Soviet Communist state in Manchuria mostly with the Koreans who were residents of northeast Manchuria at the time.[1] Chiang Kai-shek himself did not attempt to suppress such a movement, and was actually relieved when Japan moved in there.

The timing of the Japanese invasion happened at a time when there were difficulties and conflicts within Japan. The continuous struggle between military and civilian interests had intensified since the Washington Conference in 1921–1922. Under the pressures of world opinion, the big powers, the United Kingdom, the United States, France, and Japan assembled to negotiate three major treaties in order to control a full-scale naval race, immediately following the conclusion of World War I.

Japan Gains Territory at Versailles

After the Treaty of Versailles, Japan had gained two important rewards as a member of the winning team. The Americans supported their claim over the Chinese Shantung peninsula, a former German-occupied area, in the Lan sing-Ishii agreements.

Another Japanese gain as a result of the war was that Japan would control certain Pacific islands including the Marianas, the Marshalls, and the Carolines, formerly German-held islands north of the equator.

The occupation of these islands by Japan alarmed President Wilson, who had no knowledge of these secret agreements made in the treaties of 1917 without American participation. These islands located between Hawaii and the Philippines could endanger the American lines of communication between the two American naval ports.

Thus, Japanese continental expansion, the growth of Japanese naval forces, and now strategic points in the Pacific challenged the position of the United States.

The United States had taken two major policy positions in the Pacific at this time. One was to promote equal economic opportunity in China based on the Open-Door concept, and another one had been to maintain American military security in the Pacific. With the important new position of Japan, the United States became alarmed.

Washington Naval Conference

The United States invited Great Britain, Japan, France, Italy, China, Holland, Belgium, and Portugal to the naval conference in Washington in November of 1921, which lasted until February, 1922. During the conference, a Five-Power Pact on the limitation of naval armaments, a Nine-Power Pact on China, and a Four-Power Pact on the Pacific problems were discussed and negotiated.

The Five-Power Treaty, signed by the United States, Great Britain, Japan, France, and Italy, established a ratio of capital ship tonnage among the three powers. The ratio agreed upon was 5:5:3:1.75 respectively. In addition, the United States, Great Britain, and Japan agreed not to construct new naval bases or fortifications west of Hawaii, north of Singapore, or south of Japan. Under this agreement, Japan could not build new naval bases on the islands she took over from Germany.

The Washington Treaties were not well accepted by the militarists in Japan. They believed that the Western powers had tried to restrict future Japanese activities in Asia and the Pacific.

Besides the problem in the Pacific, there was another serious military problem which concerned the major powers. Japanese troops in Siberia had created an international issue. Japan sent troops to Siberia at the time of the Russian revolution in 1917. Japan was a partner of other Western powers hoping to crush the revolutionary forces in Russia. This attempt had failed. All the major powers' troops except the Japanese had withdrawn from Russia. She was trying to take advantage of Russia while the civil war was on.

Under the pressures of the major powers, Japan was eventually forced to restore the Siberian leasehold and withdraw her troops from the Shantung Province of China, and she also announced that she would withdraw from Siberia as soon as possible. In October, 1922, the last Japanese troops left the Maritime Province, although Northern Sakhalin continued to be occupied. Such conciliatory actions by their government were considered weaknesses by many Japanese, especially the army officers. As a result, the conservative Seiyukai's Takahashi cabinet fell in June, 1922. Neither Hara nor Takahashi was able to bring about the prestige of the Diet despite their advocacy of party politics.

The genro appointed Admiral Kato Tomosaburo, instead of a civilian party man, as the premier.

The genro undoubtedly believed that only a military man could carry out the disarmament program of the Washington Conference as well as fulfill the Japanese commitment to withdraw troops from Siberia. The genro, or elder statesmen, actually ruled Japan for the last twenty years of the nineteenth century and the first twenty-five years of the twentieth century. Seven of them were former Samurai from Satsuma and Choshu, and the eighth member was Saionji, a lonely court noble, the last member of the group. They answered all the important questions on behalf of the emperor. Field Marshal Prince Yamagata, until his death in 1922, dominated the military affairs as a member of Genroin or the council of elder statesmen.

Meantime, the political party men, Takahashi, Kato, Inukai, immediately decided to organize a coalition movement to force a return to party cabinets. In this they were joined by the Tokyo newspapermen.

A new election held in May 1924 was an overwhelming victory for the coalition. The Japanese people supported party-oriented politics rather than the military's aggressive attitude. With the mandate from the people, the civilian government cut four divisions from the army. War Minister Ugaki handled this with care, setting up Reserve Officer Training Corps at the colleges and universities, and modernizing the army with the money saved on cuts. In the field of foreign policy, Premier Shidehara followed a peaceful economic expansion policy against the army's will. He also established a normal relationship with Soviet Russia. In 1925, a Soviet-Japanese treaty was signed. It provided for Japan to withdraw troops from northern Sakhalin, granted fishing rights, adjusted Czarist debts, and received oil, coal, and timber concessions. Both countries promised not to engage in damaging propaganda activities.

In 1920, the economic boom that the war had created and postwar reconstruction sustained finally came to an end. When prices began to fall, the government intervened and, by authorizing the Bank of Japan to make substantial loans, halted the downward trend. The government hoped that, given time, these debts could be gradually adjusted and a crisis avoided. As a result of this policy, prices were maintained at a level above the rest of the world. Consequently, exports declined while imports increased, causing Japan great difficulties in balancing her foreign trade accounts. The civilian government was very anxious to reduce government expenditures and balance the budget. The government was unable to solve the financial crisis.

The Bank of Formosa and thirty-five other banks had to close their doors. Then the Bank of Japan, the central bank, lent 700 million yen to the failing banks. As a result of the financial crisis, two major events took place in the world of finance. First of all, the crisis eliminated many small and medium-sized companies, and secondly, it strengthened the zaibatsu's monopolistic position more than ever.

To combat capitalism with its emphasis on open competition, and Western-style, party-oriented politics, numerous ultranationalistic movements emerged. These became the strong supporters of militarism, reactionary groups who were against capitalism, the party-oriented government, and the zaibatsu system. They advocated the use of violence to overthrow the government.

Tanaka Advocates Aggression

The Mitsui house supported the Tanaka cabinet, organized around a major slogan of strong policy toward China. Tanaka was a general. He advocated an anti-Communist policy. The freedom of the Communists was not allowed, and the press was strictly censored. He maintained a protective tariff policy, economic self-sufficiency, and so forth. Above all, he wanted more colonies. General Tanaka became the leader of an aggressive military party which formulated the Positive Policy set down in the Tanaka Memorial.

This memorial was the product of a conference held in Mukden, Manchuria, in July, 1927. All civil and military officials of Manchuria and Mongolia attended. The memorial was supposed to have been the new policy of Japan drawn by this group, although there is some doubt as to its source. The memorial itself went into detail explaining the reasons and means by which Japan would first take over Manchuria, then China, and eventually all of the Far East. The basic ideas and aims behind the memorial are expressed in the following:

> Final success belongs to the country having a food supply; industrial prosperity belongs to the country having raw materials; the full growth of national strength belongs to the country having extensive territory. If we pursue a positive policy to enlarge our rights in Manchuria and China, all these prerequisites of a powerful nation will constitute no problem.[2]

The significance of this document lies in the fact that the steps which Japan followed in her aggression against first Manchuria and then China are exactly the steps which are stated in the memorial. One of the causes of World War II might well have been Japan's striving for the ultimate objective stated in the memorial.

The positive policy of Tanaka did not coincide with the liberal policy, which was known as the Shidehara policy. The liberal policy meant primarily peaceful coexistence with China, disarmament, and conciliation. It was advocated by Baron Shidehara, twice foreign minister from 1924–1927 and 1929–1931. The better climate of conciliation during this period can be traced to the decline of the army's influence through disarmament and reduction of defense expenditures, the Chinese boycott against Japanese goods which brought the merchants to support a more conciliatory policy, and the devastating earthquake which struck Japan in 1923. The Liberal policy wanted to maintain friendly relations with China to provide the soundest basis for an expansion of Japan's trade and the solution of its economic difficulties.

As we can see here, the internal power struggle between the military interests and the civilian interests in Japan had already influenced foreign policy in regard to Manchuria and China.

Relations with China

Prior to the Mukden Incident which served as the starting point for actual Japanese military aggression, there had been considerable friction between China and Japan. The Japanese felt that they couldn't retire from Manchuria due to the large capital investments made to extract natural resources, especially iron, and also her investments in the South Manchurian

Railroad. China, on the other hand, had been irritated over the Japanese position in Manchuria although she was not strong enough to challenge Japan. The Chinese were building competing railroad lines in Manchuria in an attempt to take commerce away from the Japanese-controlled ports in Manchuria, to take it south through the Chinese port of Halutao instead of through Japan's Dairen and Port Arthur. Japan obviously did not approve of this action.

The political revolution that brought about the end of the Manchu dynasty by Sun Yat-sen and his associates did not unify China. The revolution had been well-prepared for by the decline of the corrupt Manchu dynasty and the emergence of regional warlords. Weakened by its loss of control and in conflict with the provinces, the Manchu dynasty collapsed when the fight for regional autonomy turned into an attack against the Peking regime itself. The Republic of China was born in 1911, but the nation was still divided.

Leaders of regional military organizations and cliques fought among themselves for power and for control of the central government. For a time the conflict in the north focused on three warlords—Chang Tso-lin in Manchuria, Wu Pei-fu of Central China, and Feng Yu-hsiang of the Northwest. Each of these three enjoyed special foreign support. For instance, Chang Tso-lin from Japan; Wu Pei-fu from Great Britain, the United States, and France; Feng Yu-hsiang from Russia, all for different interests, but the same reason. None of them was receiving popular support from the Chinese, and none had a program to offer. One common ground among the three warlords was that they were against the revolutionary China of Sun Yat-sen.

At this time of national chaos, the Chinese progressives were greatly impressed by the news of the Russian Revolution. In 1921 the Chinese Communist Party was organized in Shanghai. In 1923, Adolph Joffe, a top diplomat, came from the Soviet Union to give public lectures at Peking University. Joffe met Sun Yat-sen in Shanghai where they concluded an agreement for Soviet support of Sun's organization. It was not to establish Communist China but to fight against Western imperialism, according to the terms of their agreement. One significant point of the agreement was that the leadership of the national revolution of China was to be in the hands of the Kuomintang, whose policies the Communists were to support.

With the death of Sun Yat-sen, the Kuomintang-Communist Alliance, however, broke down. Chiang Kai-shek became the successor of Sun Yat-sen, although three were some serious contenders among the close associates of the founder of the Republic of China. Chiang immediately started a northern expedition in the summer of 1926 in order to bring northern China into the Republic.

Chiang Seeks to Unite China

The success of the march north had given the Kuomintang a new importance in the eyes of the Chinese people as well as the Western powers. Among the Western powers, Great Britain, in particular, was eager now to support Chiang Kai-shek, provided he split with the Communist members of the Kuomintang. Chiang, a conservative nationalist, had no difficulty doing that. Chiang had received the support of the British and other foreign communities and of the Chinese businessmen, including the important Shanghai bankers. As a matter of fact, Chiang divorced his wife and married one of the three Soong sisters from the powerful banking family in Shanghai, Mei-ling. Chiang Kai-shek established the new government's capital at Nanking with his conservative support. Meanwhile, the Communists were expelled from the Kuomintang, and the Soviet advisers had left China.

When the Nationalist government was established at Nanking, there still remained the task of continuing the march north and crushing the power of Chang Tso-lin, who still controlled the government of Peking and Manchuria.

The reason that there was peace as long as there was was that Manchuria under Chang Tso-lin was more stable than the rest of war-torn China. The Japanese had secretly been using Chang Tso-lin as a friendly agent to protect their special interests in North China and Manchuria. All this ended in the spring of 1928 as the Nationalist Kuomintang army under Chiang Kai-shek moved north to force Chang Tso-lin to unite with the rest of China. Chang Tso-lin fled farther north to Manchuria and was assassinated by the Japanese, who mined a bridge over which he was travelling.

This assassination had been planned by the Japanese Kwantung Army on the theory that Chang was an unreliable ally. But in reality, they had hoped that the conflict that followed could be used as an opportunity to conquer Manchuria. Actually, their plan backfired with several bad effects. Namely, the Tanaka government in Japan fell from power, and when Chang's son, Chang Hsüeh-liang, took over in Manchuria, he immediately joined the Nationalist forces, so that the Japanese had to deal with Nanking on any question dealing with Manchuria rather than with local Mukden where they could use force to get their way.

In addition to the conflicts mentioned, there were many more. The Wanpaoshan and Nakamura affairs of June 1931 were two. The first involved the illegal digging of irrigation ditches by Koreans on land in Manchuria leased from the Chinese. The ditches were eventually completed under Japanese police protection. The Nakamura incident concerned the arrest and execution of a Japanese officer by the Chinese for alleged espionage in the interior of Manchuria.

The Mukden Incident took place on the night of September 18, 1931. By dawn, the town of Mukden was completely in the hands of the Japanese Kwantung Army. The lightning-like invasion showed that the incident had been carefully planned by a group of Kwantung Japanese Army officers with the help of the Army General staff in Tokyo, but not with the approval or knowledge of the cabinet.

Emergence of Military Elite

Therefore, the Mukden Incident was a significant departure from usual politics of aggression. It was more than just another aggressive act. It was a test of strength between the radical army leaders and the government as to which one would determine policy. On this issue, the government yielded as it would continue to do during the next several years until the militarists gained complete control. The excuse the government offered at this time was that nothing should be done to lower the prestige of the army, but in actuality they were yielding because they didn't have the power to enforce any disciplinary action.

While the action by the Kwantung Army was being discussed at home, the army was rapidly advancing into China in the three provinces of Manchuria, Kirin, Liaoning, and Heilungkiang. After the initial retreat, Marshall Chang set up his headquarters at the city of Chinchow in Manchuria. This was bombed on October 8 by Japanese planes from Mukden. The decisive battle was fought near Chinchow on January 4, 1932, when Young Marshall, during offensive action directed toward recapturing Mukden, was defeated and soon driven to the other side of the Great Wall. This battle was important because it assured the separatist movement that he wouldn't "come back."

When the Japanese army struck in Manchuria in violation of the Washington Treaties and of the Pact of Paris on September 19, 1931, the League of Nations approached the problem by trying first to secure withdrawal of troops on both sides as a condition for negotiation. When this did not work, the League set a time limit for a withdrawal of Japanese troops to the railroad zones. This did not work either.

Japan had no intention of compromising in any manner. The Japanese government was planning to separate Manchuria from China, and was ready to set up an independent puppet state, known as Manchukuo. Consequently, Japan could now press the independence movement, which she had been working toward, to its conclusion. The complete conquest of Manchuria came with the seizure of Harbin on February 5, 1932.

The government in Tokyo was obviously alarmed by the Kwantung Army's independent action in northern China and Manchuria. The best thing the authority, in this case the only remaining genro, Saionji, could do was to replace the premier. Premier Tanaka was replaced by Hamaguchi, the leader of the Minseitō Party, supported by the Mitsubishi house. Hamaguchi advocated 1) conciliatory policy toward China; 2) disarmament; 3) a strong economy; 4) elimination of corruption. However, the time was not right for him.

In 1930, silk prices fell by 50 percent and overall exports dropped 27 percent. Consequently, the peasants of Japan were in a desperate plight. The situation worsened as evidenced by a decline in production of goods, especially rice. Hamaguchi went ahead to the London Naval Reduction Treaty in 1930, cut more armed forces, as well as their salaries. Such drastic actions disturbed the army more than any other single group in Japan. He was assassinated by a fanatic in November.

On May 15, 1932, again, young naval and army officers attacked police headquarters in Tokyo, also banks and party offices. After murdering premier Inukai, they surrendered voluntarily to the police. A public trial followed.

During the public trial which the young militarists had demanded, their ideas were announced to the Japanese people. The young fanatics explained that the nation could be saved only by destroying Japan's Western-oriented political system, including political parties, the bureaucracy, Diet, cabinet, and so forth. They also stressed that the zaibatsu economic system was responsible for the corruption and decay of modern Japan. Due to the ruling class of modern Japan, they explained, the nation was suffering, especially the farmers. The public reaction to the trials, which were extensively reported in the press, was one of sympathy and many saw the assassins as national heroes. Even the prosecutors treated the young rebels as if they had committed patriotic acts. As a result, the militarists were more than encouraged. The party leaders, on the other hand, were intimidated by the terroristic acts of the radical militarists. The political tide had obviously turned against them and the establishment in general.

For example, when the Japanese army, which had been stationed in Kwantung, invaded Manchuria, referred to as the Mukden Incident, the government in Tokyo was forced to accept the invasion of China as a legitimate action. Not only did Tokyo defend the army's violent action, but eventually established Manchukuo as a puppet state. The Manchurian Incident was the Kwantung Army's independent action taken without the Tokyo government's approval. The government, however, eventually had to yield to the army. It did not dare propose disciplinary action, because it could not possibly enforce it.

Goals for Manchukuo

The military radicals believed that they had found their utopia in Manchukuo. This new state was to be without capitalists and without party politicians, a pilot project for a new Japan they dreamed of. The army began to plan and develop a continental war base in Manchukuo, a first step in the plan to take over all of Asia.

The creation of Manchukuo destroyed any hope that there might have been peaceful relations with Nationalist China. China appealed to the League of Nations, the Pact of Paris, the Washington Treaty Nations, and other peace-keeping organizations. Eventually all of this machinery was invoked but did not deter Japan from the path chosen by the Kwantung Army radicals. Japan took over almost entirely the British argument as it was voiced in the *London Times.* British opinion, at least in the *Times'* editorial, sympathized with Japan's position. After all, there were no British interests in Manchuria. The British expressed their concern only after Japan attacked Shanghai, because of major British commercial interests there.

Meanwhile, in January, Shanghai became the scene of an upsurge of Chinese Nationalist sentiment which led to a rigid boycotting of Japanese goods and services, which within three months led to a one-third cut in Japan's exports to China. The Japanese couldn't afford this reduction, so when a mob of Chinese attacked five Buddhist Japanese priests on a downtown street, Shanghai residents took revenge. In the melee, a Chinese policeman and a Japanese soldier were killed. Admiral Yamamoto of the Japanese navy, who hadn't participated in any of the aggression in China up to this point, said he was not satisfied with the attitude of the local Chinese authorities and threatened to begin hostilities if things were not straightened out.

Hostilities began in the Chapei district of Shanghai, which the Chinese Nationalists had been ordered to vacate. But the order had been ignored. The next day, carrier-based Japanese planes began bombing Shanghai. The Chinese 19th Route Army under the leadership of a Cantonese general put up strong resistance until March 3, 1932, when they were forced to retreat to a specified area outside the city. The incident ended with a local armistice arranged with international assistance on May 5, 1932. By its stipulations, the Chinese government agreed not to fortify the Chinese section of Shanghai. Thus Shanghai became a demilitarized zone.

China Cries for Help

During the period that began with the Mukden Incident, the Chinese had appealed more than once to the League of Nations. The first League action was to pass a resolution immediately advising both sides to withdraw their troops and to cease fighting. The Japanese, in reply to this, objected to intervention by the League and declared a preference for negotiations directly with the Chinese. The Chinese, in turn, refused to engage in bilateral negotiations as long as Japanese soldiers occupied Manchuria outside of railroad zones. It was at this point in December 1931, with neither side willing to negotiate, that the League sent Lord Lytton as head of a commission to investigate the situation.

There were several different views and ideas about the League action, but most seem to indicate that it accomplished little and history has since proved that it accomplished nothing. Agnes Smedley in *Battle Hymn of China* stated that the sending of the Commission to "investigate" the situation indicated a belief that the news dispatches reporting the invasion of Manchuria were just fabrications of the Chinese. She then went on to say that anyone who had read *The Tanaka Memorial* would notice that the invasion of Manchuria was one of the first steps in Japan's plan of empire.[3]

In his book, *Manchukuo Child of Conflict,* K. K. Kawahami, Washington correspondent of *The Tokyo Hochi Shimbun*, stated his thoughts on the Commission Report. His main point was also brought out in the Lytton Report, that almost all the conditions recommended by the Commission were based on the setting up of a strong central government in China, which he, in turn, said could only be done with the assistance of Japan and other powers over a long period of time. He stated that it would be impossible to expect a local police force to maintain order in a country as large as Manchuria. This remark was made concerning the point in the Report stating that a gendarmerie force should replace the Chinese and Japanese armies. He also stated that if the League had taken that stand soon after the Mukden Incident instead of a year and a half later, Japan would have been more than willing to negotiate. The following are the points to which he referred in his statement:

> First, that the Sino-Japanese treaties which existed in September, 1931, are binding on both Signatories.
>
> Second, that anti-foreign and in this particular case anti-Japanese boycott employed by China involved a measure of Chinese government responsibility.
>
> Third, nowhere in the report does the Commission suggest that the Japanese troops be withdrawn as a prerequisite of negotiations between China and Japan on the basis of the above two principles.

It is interesting to note that he didn't say the basis of the report in general. On the contrary, it suggests the organization of an effective gendarmerie force as a preliminary step to troop withdrawal.[4] The book was published in 1933 but history has proved that Japan's aim at this time and for the next ten years was expansion in the Pacific and Far East, and although it may have been the opinion of that author that Japan would give up her position in Manchuria, it is doubtful that the militarists in Japan would ever have permitted the return of Manchuria to its former relationship with China.

On October 2, 1932, the Lytton Commission, appointed by the League of Nations to investigate the Sino-Japanese dispute, published a report that stated in general that Japan's action in Manchuria was not one of self-defense and that the creation of Manchukuo was not a genuine and spontaneous movement. The Commission also recommended that an autonomous government under the sovereignty of China be established. The government was to be equipped with a police force with which to help keep the government running properly; after a stable government was set up in Manchuria, China would pledge to recognize Japan's rights and interests there. The recommendations of the Lytton Commission made good sense, but there were many problems that had to be overcome first.

Weakness of League

A major problem was that neither country had approved the plan. The Chinese Nationalists were against any plan that left foreign powers entrenched on Chinese territory, especially the Japanese railroads in Manchuria. The Japanese, in turn, said they had acted in self-defense in protecting their treaty rights against the encroachments of the Chinese Nationalists from the south. Japan also stated that she was protecting the subjugated people of Manchuria from the cruel Chinese tyrants. Most of the sentiment was on the side of the Chinese, and on February 24, 1933, the League of Nations approved the Lytton Report.

In spite of the sympathetic attitude of the Commission's report, which acknowledged a legitimate right of Japan in Manchuria, Japan withdrew from the League of Nations in protest.

There were other problems facing the League, especially because it had no power to enforce the stand it had taken. The League needed the support of Great Britain and the United States. However, both these countries were preoccupied with problems at home and not especially interested in Manchuria. The United States as well as the rest of the world was in the middle of a serious depression. Much of the world was in a state of turmoil. The Japanese attacks in Manchuria and at Shanghai and the resulting Manchukuo government were a challenge to the Open Door Policy which the United States had supported. Although it was in direct conflict with this avowed policy, there was much support among the American people for a neutral policy, noninvolvement in foreign affairs, and without American support, the British didn't want to become involved either.

What justification did Japan need to have in order to invade Manchuria? Actually Manchuria had been divided into two general spheres of interest, Japanese and Russian, ever since the Russo-Japanese War of 1904–1905. Russia's hold was in the north but considerably weakened by the Russian Revolution of 1917. The Japanese controlled the Liaotung Peninsula, including Port Arthur and Dairen, and the zone of the Southern Manchurian Railroad. Japan valued Manchuria greatly. It was her economic life line. The Japanese were very disturbed when China tried to assert authority in Manchuria. But China had, by then, become stronger under Chiang Kai-shek and the Kuomintang (Nationalist) Party. Chiang drove north from Canton to the Yangtze Valley and he established his governmental headquarters at Nanking. Japan was faced with a somewhat united and stronger China that objected to Japan's authority in Manchuria. This situation was all that Japan's military clique needed.

In 1931, the Japanese press published stories of Chinese attacks on Korean farmers who were then Japanese subjects. Even of more serious consequence was the killing by the Chinese of Captain Nakamura, whose purpose in China was espionage. The Japanese government under Prime Minister Wakatsuki and Foreign Minister Shidehara was negotiating with the Chinese in an attempt to prevent any conflict. But the military created another dilemma. On September 18, 1931, a section of track of the Southern Manchurian Railway was sabotaged. The extent of the damage was very slight but the Japanese immediately accused the Chinese and within a few hours, the Japanese had seized the Chinese stronghold of Mukden and other key points along the railroad. This action was taken solely by the military, acting independently of the civilian government.

The civilian government of Tokyo pledged to remove the troops as soon as possible, but the military interests were not willing to follow Prime Minister Wakatsuki's wishes. The Japanese military group had not moved out of Manchuria before nor did it intend to.

These aggressive actions violated the League's Covenant, the Washington Treaty, and the Kellogg-Briand Pact, in which Japan had agreed to respect the political and territorial rights of China.

The Japanese militarists evidently had no fear of confronting the United States or the League of Nations. After all, it was Secretary of State Henry Stimson who made the strongest statement against the Japanese aggression. His statement declared that the American government "cannot admit the legality of any situation de facto nor does it intend to recognize any treaty or agreement entered into between those governments or agents thereof, which may impair the treaty rights of the United States or its citizens in China, including those which relate to the sovereignty, the independence, or the territorial and administrative integrity of the Republic of China, or to the international policy relative to China commonly known as the Open Door Policy; and that it does not intend to recognize any situation, treaty, or agreement which may be brought about by means contrary to the Pact of Paris."[5]

The main points of the nonrecognition statement are as follows:

> First: it was a moral sanction designed to let the friends of the United States in China know that although the United States could not prevent Japan's aggression against them, at least there was no doubt about how it felt on the subject.
>
> Second: nonrecognition represented a reinforcement of the international treaty structure, especially the Kellogg-Briand Pact to which Stimson's note referred.
>
> Third: the doctrine expressed the feelings of the American people that Japan's aggression was wrong.

The Kellogg-Briand Pact had been signed on August 27, 1928, by fifteen nations and later by many more. It grew out of a proposed treaty between France and the United States to prohibit war between those two countries and later expanded to condemn all wars. The Pact "condemns recourse to war for the solution of international controversies, and renounces it as an instrument of national policy in their relationships with one another." It also stated that "settlement of disputes shall never be sought except by specific means."

Nonrecognition Policy

During this entire period, except for the Japanese attack on Shanghai, the British would not support Stimson's doctrine of nonrecognition, using the excuse that Britain, as a member of the League, should not act independently of League action. Stimson stated that the Japanese were more afraid of Anglo-American cooperation than the whole League, but he got no British backing, and the only force shown was moving the entire United States Pacific fleet to Hawaii in February, 1932.

Soon afterward, a letter exchanged between Stimson and Senator William Borah was published; this letter stressed the historical development of United States policy toward China during this century, especially in regard to the nine-power treaty of Washington and the Kellogg-Briand Pact. It also declared that the events in Manchuria and Shanghai should convince other powers that active support of this covenant was necessary and that the nonrecognition policy of the United States was the way to accomplish this. There were, during 1932 and later, a number of attempts in the United States to put economic sanctions on paper, but President Hoover opposed them. Nevertheless, Stimson was in favor of this move because he realized that in letting Japan have her way in Manchuria, the United States would be endangering her own trade, as well as her position in the Pacific. However, the only sanction President Hoover would permit was one of adverse public opinion. Hoover also said that if the League of Nations would impose an economic sanction, the United States would not interfere. The smaller members of the League were in favor of an economic sanction, but it was opposed by the larger members who had the burden of enforcing it.

Again, under the administration of Franklin D. Roosevelt, the policy was to welcome trade with the Japanese and also with Manchukuo, but nothing was to be done about the situation in the Far East. The United States maintained a strong isolationist position until 1932, with people holding the same views they had held during the controversies over whether or not to join the League. There was also a feeling that the so-called "merchants of death" or munitions manufacturers had started World War I, which led to strong pacifist sentiments.

On February 24, 1933, the same day as approval of the Lytton report and the statement of the United States' nonrecognition policy was granted by the League, the Japanese delegation walked out of the Assembly. On March 27, 1933, an Imperial Rescript was issued which proclaimed Japan's official resignation from the League. The Rescript also was the basis of Japan's foreign policy. It said that, although Japan had left the League of Nations, she would continue to cooperate internationally in the hope of maintaining peace. It also stated that Japan would respect the independence of Manchukuo and would encourage its development.

On May 25, 1933, the Tangku armistice agreement was signed between the Nanking government and the Japanese, and brought an end to hostility over Manchuria itself. At the time of the signing of the Truce, the Japanese had control of Kirin, Liaoning, Heilungkiang, and Jehol provinces in China and had armies operating in the area south of the Great Wall. By this truce, the Japanese troops were to withdraw to Manchukuo, and the Chinese forces were to move farther south, leaving a demilitarized neutral zone in which the Chinese were to maintain order through use of a police force.

There was also a clause in the truce which said that it was necessary for China to preserve order before it would become mandatory for the Japanese to leave. This clause was used later, when Japan renewed her aggression, as an excuse for her action. One authority stated that Japan signed the truce "because time was needed to consolidate and organize the base in Manchukuo preparatory to the next advances in China."[6] Japan established in Manchukuo an orderly and efficient administration on the continent of Asia, a defense bastion, a base for military operations that would contribute to the strength and glorification of Japan for ages.

In early 1932, Japan officially announced the creation of the new state of Manchukuo headed by puppet Henri Pu-yi, the last emperor of the Manchu Dynasty. Pu-yi had abdicated in 1912 after the Chinese revolution overthrew the Manchus and created the Republic of China. The new "independent" state of Manchukuo included the three northeastern provinces and the province of Jehol in north China. This change in the form of government meant increased centralization of administration, fewer civil rights, and stricter control by the Japanese of Manchukuo. The highest authority in the new government was lodged in the new official position which combined the posts of the Japanese ambassador, the commander-in-chief of the Kwantung Army, and the governor of the Kwantung area.

Manchukuo first addressed itself to the problems of law and order. The government used the army, the police, and a home guard for pacification, undertook modest agricultural relief programs, and offered pardons to those who would surrender or reform. Manchukuo pioneered in coping with problems which paralleled the Hukbalahaps[7] later in the Philippines and the Communist guerillas in the jungles of Malaya. When mild measures failed, the government herded the farmers into protected villages, registered all the inhabitants, and held the household rather than individuals responsible for any person carrying weapons, creating public disturbances, or suspected of bandit activities. But they never were able to control them in spite of villages deliberately burned.

Manchukuo's arguments with its northern and western neighbors added to its instability. During this period, Soviet Russia was following a policy of peace at almost any price, so the irritations provoked by the Manchukuo government did not lead to outright war. There were about 2300 border disputes between 1934–1937, according to Foreign Minister Hayashi. Thus, Japan had defied the League of Nations, rejected her treaty commitments, and ignored any peaceful approach to the settlement in China. Japan had escaped punishment and other aggressive powers were soon to follow the same pattern. Mussolini's Italy invaded Ethiopia, and Hitler started war in Europe.

It has been clearly demonstrated by these events that Japanese military aggression could take place without the civilian government's approval and popular support. A small fraction of the Kwantung Japanese Army succeeded in initiating war against China although the Tokyo government had attempted to maintain peace. Baron Shidehara's policy had, at least, demonstrated such an intention.

Notes

1. Sunoo, *Korea,* pp. 249–251.

2. Giichi Tanaka, *The Tanaka Memorial* (New York. International Publishers, 1942).

3. Agnes Smedley, *Battle Hymn of China* (New York: Blackiston, 1943), p. 102.

4. Ibid., pp. 1–7.

5. T. A. Bisson, *America's Far Eastern Policy* (New York: Macmillan, 1945), p. 32.

6. Claude A. Buss, *The Far East* (New York: Macmillan, 1938), p. 222.

7. Hukbalahaps or the Anti-Japanese Resistance Society was organized during the Japanese occupation in the Philippines in 1943. The Japanese army, together with the Japanese concerns, exploited the Philippines with the assistance of Philippine collaborators. Most of the guerillas, however, were tenant farmers, and they fought against both the Japanese and the collaborators. The largest such organization on the island of Luzon became known as the Hukbalahaps, an abbreviation of Anti-Japanese Resistance Society. They received American support and had close contact with the American army before

the liberation. Their leader, Lui Tarue, was a known communist, and the American government made no effort to continue with the group after the liberation of the islands.

5 Defeat in World War II

The Japanese militarists gambled again but this time they lost. World War II was the first time that that nation had experienced defeat by foreign powers. The militarists had believed that Japan was invincible because it was a sacred nation whose ultimate destiny was to rule the world. These men believed that the army was the vanguard of the nation and that only the army was able to uphold the empire and promote the "imperial idea" to other countries. Their obvious aim was to build an Asiatic empire. But they failed and surrendered unconditionally to the Allied Powers.

The war against the United States came about primarily because the Japanese militarists underrated America's potential strength. It was unfortunate for Japan that shortsighted militarists controlled the government when they did. Their willingness to wage war was no match for American strength.

The downfall of the empire began psychologically, if not militarily, on April 7 1945, when the last modern Japanese battleship, the *Yamato,* was sunk near the island of Kyushu. This was the beginning of the end for the Japanese fleet. Out of an original twelve battleships, only four were left afloat, and these had all been damaged in varying degrees. Out of twenty-six aircraft carriers, including one that had not as yet been put in commission, seven remained. Only six out of eighteen heavy cruisers were left, and at least two of these were under repair. The remnants of the Japanese navy were driven into the protection of ports and dockyards, only to await attack from the air.

The End in Sight

With Japanese sea defense shattered, an added burden fell on her already hard-pressed air forces. The last faint hope of crippling the American fleet lay in the use of air power. Mounting plane losses were accompanied by damaging blows at plane production; and while output was still ahead of losses, the dwindling margin made it increasingly difficult for Japan to mount a campaign on a scale large enough to check the American amphibious advance, and at the same time accumulate adequate air reserves for the final test when the invasion would be launched against Japan itself.

The war was thus brought to Japan's home front when her naval power was shattered, and American air bases had been established on the Marianas, Guam, and other islands from which the American superfortresses could launch attacks. Japanese militarists found that political difficulties were added to their many other problems. Periodic boasts of heavy losses inflicted on the American forces, and repeated prophecies of the imminent destruction of the advancing enemy troops, failed to conceal the fact that the advance was continuing unchecked. When such boasts were alternated with urgent warnings about the increasing seriousness of the situation, these served to accentuate the complete failure of the government.

Any serious popular discontent or any widespread talk about peace could be kept under control by the police, but patriotic shouts for stronger measures of national defense were harder to suppress. By the beginning of 1945, there was a rising campaign for drastic changes in both the structure and the composition of the government. The more desperate they became, the more control was needed. Most Japanese historians agree today that Japan was a fascist society during the thirties and the forties, having moved away from parliamentary government. A narrow-minded nationalism and the terrorist techniques of the radical right contributed to bringing about authoritarianism. There was no freedom of press, speech, and assembly. Antigovernment speakers were imprisoned. Unlike the German Nazi party, the Japanese antiparliamentary forces were neither a dynamic nor united group. The new political leaders were appointed by Emperor Hirohito through his genro in order to control the army. Behind the political scenes within the establishment there were endless disputes, maneuvers, compromises, and conspiracies among the elites. The people were not only confused, but also ignorant of the whole situation. They were not told the truth about the war, and there was no way they could have been informed. The military controlled the society.

A new organization, the Political Association of Greater Japan, was formally constituted at the end of March under the leadership of the extreme militarist, General Minami, former governor-general of Korea. Its object was to press for more vigorous war measures, outside of and, if necessary, in opposition to, the government itself.

Wartime Turmoil

This unrest within the government was not unusual during World War II. Prince Konoye was the prime minister at the start of the war but had gotten cold feet at the time the United States entered the war and had resigned. His office was taken over by General Hideki Tojo, his former war minister. Tojo was all for a fight with the United States, and for the first several months after Pearl Harbor, he was a national hero in Japan. Soon, however, the tide began to turn, and after several big defeats, the United States was on the offensive. Public feeling started turning against him and grew so intense that Tojo was forced to resign.

Tojo's successor, General Koiso, was installed as prime minister in July of 1944. From the very beginning, he gave up all notions of securing an outright victory, but he did hope to prolong the fight until the enemy became tired of the conflict and then a peace could be negotiated on terms not too unfavorable to Japan.

Unfortunately for Koiso's regime, the Soviet Union denounced its neutrality pact with Japan on April 5, 1945. This pact had made it possible for Russia to throw her main strength into the European struggle. Now, however, with the war in Europe drawing to a close, the treaty's main purpose had been served as far as Russia was concerned. Japan was accused of aiding Germany as her ally in the war against Russia, and of waging war on the allies of the Soviet Union. Actually, this was probably just a formal step by Russia to free her hands for the fulfillment of her still secret Yalta pledge.

This secret agreement, made in February 1945 at Yalta, stated, "The leaders of the three great powers—the Soviet Union, the United States of America, and Great Britain—agreed that in two or three months after Germany has surrendered and the war in Europe has terminated, the Soviet Union shall enter into the war against Japan on the side of the Allies. . . ."[1]

The Koiso cabinet resigned on the same day, April 5, 1945, under the pressure of the new international development. Admiral Suzuki formed a new cabinet in which General Minami was included as a minister without portfolio. The American invasion of Okinawa was now under way.

The Japanese government had taken preliminary steps in March to provide for a fuller mobilization of manpower and resources. The new government called a special session of the Diet in June to express formal national approval of the dictatorial powers over persons and property which the premier had, in any case, a right to assume under the emergency clause of the constitution. After this session, the full resources of the nation were now at the disposal of the Suzuki-Minami government to conduct total war.

With the invasion of Okinawa by the Americans in April, 1945, the Allied Forces were ready to invade the homeland of Japan. There was growing speculation in the United States that the Japanese might be brought to submission without a land battle, but this was not taken seriously. The Japanese were determined to defend the empire at all costs under the fanatic leadership of Suzuki and Minami.

In July, the Third Fleet under Admiral Halsey's command set out on their mission of preparing the way for invasion. In this fleet were over one hundred warships and in mid-July, these were joined by a British force of twenty-eight. The objectives of this powerful armada were summed up by Admiral Nimitz, "We intend to deny the enemy use of the waters surrounding him, even down to the detail of hampering his efforts to get fish out of them."[2]

In these attacks, the Third Fleet was practically unopposed by the Japanese, probably because they were saving their planes for later emergencies.

Beginning on May 14, 1945, Japan's industrial and defense centers were hit by major air raids on an average of one every three days for the next three months. In the month that followed Tokyo, Nagoya, Osaka, Kobe, and Yokohama were raided two or three times each, and by mid-June, it was officially stated that these five cities had been effectively eliminated as far as productive targets were concerned; and while they were later the scene of attacks on special objectives, the main weight of the campaign was then directed against towns ranging in population from 30,000 to 300,000.

For the next two months, the bombers worked methodically through the list of these secondary centers of war production. By mid-August, over sixty Japanese cities had felt the weight of major air attacks.[3]

Japan no longer had the means to launch an offensive. She had to wait for the Allies to come closer and hoarded her resources for a decisive counterattack. By holding back, however, Japan succeeded in leaving her war resources open to destruction. In the absence of any hope of positive victory, the one chance lay in a successful defense which would discourage the Allies and avert the full consequences of defeat.

To attain this goal, Japan relied on the tactics of suicide attacks. In her home islands, she had an air strength of 11,000 planes and ground forces numbering over two million men. This hoarded strength was to be thrown at the invaders when they landed on Japan's shores. However, Japan was inevitably doomed and in the long run those desperate measures only made ultimate defeat more certain.

Blindness of Military Leaders

Few Japanese militarists, however, recognized that defeat was inevitable. They could not possibly entertain any thoughts of defeat. How could the imperial Japanese armed forces ever be defeated by the degenerate Americans? There was another element to be considered. Apart from the fact that the open admission of such a belief would invite assassination at the hands of patriotic extremists, racial pride and professional reputation were strong deterrents to any acknowledgment that war with the Allies had led Japan to disaster. Nevertheless, some groups were ready to explore the possibility of a negotiated peace that would save face, always so important to the Japanese, and thus eliminate any question of unconditional surrender. By July, these efforts took the more serious form of talks with Russia, suggesting the possibility of Soviet mediation. All of this, however, was too tentative and indefinite to have any effect. Far from indicating any desire for compromise, the Allies on July 26, 1945, issued a firm and explicit demand for prompt and unconditional surrender. Japan would not accept such terms.

By midsummer of 1945, the atomic bomb had become a reality. It was the first manmade explosion of atomic power and an event which ushered in a new era in world history. Ignorant as they were of the very existence of this bomb, the Japanese could hardly have been expected to recognize that the words of the Allies carried an entirely new meaning. In a statement on July 29, Premier Suzuki scornfully refused to take any official notice of the Allied ultimatum. The Allied military leaders, eager to bring the bomb into immediate use, were then left with a free hand.

The scientists who had created the new weapon were far less enthusiastic about it than the military authorities. When the bomb became a reality, a group of the scientists involved drew up a memorandum requesting that it be first used in a way that would demonstrate its power without involving any loss of life. If, for instance, it had been dropped on an uninhabited area in Japan, and if this had been coupled directly with a clearer version of the Potsdam Proclamation, it's hard to see what America could have lost. Japan would still have had no defense against the new weapon and even if the demonstration failed to bring her to reason at once, the American people would have had their conscience spared. However, if the war was allowed to continue, American military leaders said that thousands more Allied soldiers would have lost their lives due to the fanatical fighting and suicide missions of the Japanese. President Truman agreed. So, on August 6, 1945, the first atomic bomb was dropped on Hiroshima; and three days later, another of a different type and of even greater power was dropped on Nagasaki.

The results were appalling. Over half of Hiroshima was devastated and 78,000 persons killed by a single blast, and at Nagasaki, the obliteration within the area of explosion was even greater. If the Japanese had ignored the threats from Potsdam, they now had good reason for heeding the words of President Truman in his announcement of the bombing of Hiroshima: "We are now prepared to obliterate more rapidly and completely every productive enterprise the Japanese have ground in any city. . . . Let there be no mistake; we shall completely destroy Japan's power to make war."[4]

Surrender and Face-Saving

The appearance of the atomic bomb offered Japan a chance to surrender and still avoid a complete loss of face. The view could be put forward—as it actually was in the emperor's surrender proclamation—that this was a new and inhuman device which would take an uncounted toll of innocent lives and threaten the destruction of human civilization, and that humanitarian considerations rather than a sense of defeat prompted Japan's decision to end the war. The entry of Russia lent added urgency to the peace efforts. It virtually ended any serious hope that a prolonged resistance could be maintained on the Asiatic mainland, and it called for speedy action before new disasters befell the Japanese. When the military extremists continued their stubborn resistance, the question was referred to the emperor for his personal decision. He called a special meeting of the cabinet and leading statesmen; and after an all-night session on August 8, 1945, the decision was made to sue for peace.

On August 10, the Allies were informed of Japan's readiness to accept the Potsdam terms, with the proviso that the terms involve nothing prejudicial to the position of the emperor. To this qualification, the Allies replied that the emperor's authority would be subject to that of the Allied Commander, and that the ultimate form of government would be left to the free decision of the Japanese people. It actually suited the Allied purpose to have the emperor remain temporarily in power because of the obedience he commanded from the people.

The reply to the Japanese said nothing about the emperor's prerogatives except that he must accept the orders of the Allied Commander. In other words, he was to do as he was told. This response conceded little, but by implying that the emperor would at least retain his throne for the present, it allowed the Japanese to regard it as at least satisfactory in form. On August 14, 1945, the emperor announced Japan's unconditional surrender.

Some 1,850,000 Japanese had been killed in the war, not counting the casualties of Hiroshima and Nagasaki. Forty percent of Japan's urban area was destroyed or damaged, with about 2,252,000 buildings destroyed. Inflation climbed as the government paid off war workers. Black market operations increased. At times it became necessary for law-abiding Japanese to buy from illegal sellers. The damage to self-respect and morale was great. Only the peasants seemed to escape. With the urban economy virtually at a standstill, the peasant found himself better off than ever before. His house was intact and the demands for his products were great. Still this small ray of light did not make the overall picture of Japan any less bleak.

After the war, Prince Higashikuni, who was from the Imperial family, became premier. In his first address to the people, he stressed the necessity of carrying out the surrender terms in order to regain the confidence of the world. He urged the people not to fall into depression and defeatism, but to pick up the pieces and work hard to restore the country and once again be in a position of power and prestige. Responding to his plea, the Japanese people, with whom neatness is a way of life, began bravely and almost happily the huge task of cleaning up the piles of destruction.

The Japanese have always shown an amazing quality for adaptation, change, and acceptance. The occupation was received with an amazing lack of outward resentment. For the most part, the Japanese swallowed their defeat, though it was hard to swallow, and looked to the future to see how best they could get back on their feet.

Notes

1. Richard Lauterback, *Danger From the East* (New York: Harper, 1947), p. 389.

2. *Encyclopaedia Britannica,* "World War II," 23:793A.

3. Thorsten Kalijarvi, "Peace Settlements of World War II," *Annals,* Vol. 257 (Philadelphia: American Academy of Political and Social Science, 1948), p. 24.

4. Edgar McInnis, *The War: Sixth Year* (Toronto: Oxford Press, 1946), p. 278.

6 The Occupation

The occupation of Japan was planned and executed as the sole responsibility of America. The United States had had enough trouble with the Soviet Union during the German occupation, so they were not eager to repeat that experience. Furthermore, the struggle against Japan had been almost entirely an American fight. Assistance from the Soviet Union had been unnecessary. Additionally, America regarded the Far East as an arena in which important changes were taking place. The United States believed that the old colonial empires would be replaced by new kinds of nationalism and intended to play a major role in this process. America had no intention of relaxing its vigilance in Asia after the war.

The first steps in shaping the occupation policy were taken in several conferences held before the end of the war at Cairo, Potsdam, Moscow, and Yalta. Starting in 1943, the leaders of the Allied nations met to consider various procedures and policies to pursue after the destruction of the Axis powers. In November 1943, Roosevelt, Churchill, and Chiang Kai-shek met in Cairo, the first of several such conferences. This was followed by a similar one at Yalta in February 1945 between

Churchill, Roosevelt, and Stalin. The text of the two conferences may be summarized in the statement that the Big Four Powers had "pledged a Japan without empire." The same three men who conferred in Cairo in 1943 had convened at Potsdam on July 17, 1945. The Soviet Union had adhered to the policy agreed on at Potsdam when it finally declared war on Japan, August 8, 1945.[1]

Occupation Policy Set

The occupation policy was stated officially in the Potsdam Declaration of July 27, 1945, which gave Japan its last chance to avoid total destruction. The Potsdam Declaration said that the Japanese had to submit to occupation for an unspecified period of time and had to institute both economic and social reforms, or face total annihilation.

According to the terms, "the authority and influence of those who have deceived and misled the people of Japan into embarking on world conquest" were to be eliminated for all time. Here is basically what it said:

> The following are our terms: we will not deviate from them; there are no alternatives; we shall brook no delay.
>
> There must be eliminated for all time the authority and influence of those who have deceived and misled the people of Japan into embarking on world conquest, for we insist that a new order of peace, security, and justice will be impossible until irresponsible militarism is driven from the world.
>
> Until such a new order is established and until there is convincing proof that Japan's war-making power is destroyed, points in Japanese territory to be designated by the Allies shall be occupied to secure the achievement of the basic objectives we are here setting forth.
>
> We do not intend that the Japanese shall be enslaved as a race or destroyed as a nation, but stern justice shall be meted out to all war criminals, including those who have visited cruelties upon our prisoners. The Japanese government shall remove all obstacles to the revival and strengthening of democratic tendencies among the Japanese people. Freedom of speech and religion and of

> thought, as well as respect for the fundamental human rights, shall be established.
>
> Japan shall be permitted to maintain such industries as will sustain her economy and permit the payment of just reparation in kind, but not those industries which will enable her to rearm for war. To this end access to, as distinguished from control of, raw materials shall be permitted. Eventual Japanese participation in world trade relations shall be permitted.
>
> The occupying forces of the Allies shall be withdrawn from Japan as these objectives have been accomplished and there has been established in accordance with the freely expressed will of the Japanese people a peacefully inclined and responsible Government.
>
> We call upon the Government of Japan to proclaim now the unconditional surrender of all Japanese armed forces, and to provide proper and adequate assurances of their good faith in such action. The alternative for Japan is prompt and utter destruction.[2]

One major part of the occupational policy was the "indication that the Allies would work in some fashion through a continuing Japanese state." The Potsdam Declaration had been accepted easily by the United States, as it seemed to fit with previous American policy. This could be seen in the ideas of returning full sovereignty to Japan and establishing several reforms that would enable her to regain status in the world community.

Five months after the Potsdam Conference, the thirteen nations who had fought for the Allies met in Moscow. The most significant result of the Moscow Conference was establishing the Far Eastern Commission, which met in December of 1945 for the first time. The Far Eastern Commission was "to formulate the policies, principles, and standards of conformity with which the fulfillment by Japan of its obligations under the terms of the surrender might be accomplished." The Far Eastern Commission then met in Washington, D.C., with representatives from the eleven Allied nations: the United States, United Kingdom, Soviet Union, China, France, Netherlands, Canada, Australia, New Zealand, India, and the Philippines.

Its function was to adopt policy decisions, which were to be transmitted to the Supreme Allied Commander through the United States government. Although the commission did on certain occasions follow an independent course, it more frequently formed its policy to conform with that of the United States.

At the meeting in Moscow, an Allied Council was set up to consult and advise the Supreme Commander. The Allied Council was composed of four nations: the United States, the Soviet Union, China, and the United Kingdom. The chairman was to be the Supreme Commander or his deputy.

MacArthur Takes Command

The individual responsible for the administration of these occupation policies was General Douglas MacArthur, named the Supreme Commander for the Allied Forces by President Truman. General MacArthur, as well as heading an international organization, had also been the commander-in-chief of the United States forces in the Far Eastern Command. The great conflict he faced as he took charge of the occupation of Japan was in deciding to whom he was to be responsible. Two weeks after his appointment, MacArthur issued his first statement regarding the Japanese occupation:

> Military control of Japan will be established by the Commander-in-Chief as the Supreme Commander for the Allied Powers.
>
> The Supreme Commander for the Allied Powers will exercise control over Japan and the Japanese, to the greatest practical extent, through the Emperor and the various instrumentalities of the Japanese Imperial government which prove suitable for this purpose.
>
> The Supreme Commander for the Allied Powers will issue all necessary instructions to the Japanese Emperor or to the Imperial Government and every opportunity will be given for the government and the Japanese people to carry out such instructions without further compulsion. If necessary, however, the Supreme Commander will issue appropriate orders to the army and Government or the Japanese people within the areas of their command. In

> other words, the occupational forces will act principally as an agency upon which the Supreme Commander may call, if necessary, to secure compliance with his instructions to the Japanese Imperial Government.[3]

On the twenty-ninth of August, 1945, a presidential paper drafted for the guidance of General MacArthur was issued by the United States. Labeled as the United States Initial Post-Surrender Policy, it was the most elaborate definition of the occupational objectives yet published. The policy stated that the United States' aims and objectives were to be carried out with the Japanese government and people both being subject to the edicts of the Supreme Commander. He was to exercise policy through the Japanese people to the fullest extent possible, but retained the power to make changes in governmental structure, personnel, and policy, and to aid directly, if necessary, to further the policies of the United States. The most significant statement was:

> The policy is to use the existing form of government in Japan, not to support it. Changes in the form of government initiated by the Japanese people or government in the direction of modifying its feudal act of authoritarian tendencies are to be permitted and favored. In the event that the effectuation of such change involves the use of force by the Japanese people or government against persons opposed thereto, the Supreme Commander should intervene only where necessary to insure the security of his forces and the attainment of all other objectives of the occupation.[4]

As one can easily see, American policy called for a supervised revolution in Japan. The policy statement outlined the ultimate objectives of the occupation so as "to insure that Japan will never again become a menace to the United States or to the peace and security of the world, and to bring about the eventual establishment of a peaceful and responsible government which will respect the rights of other states." To this last, the noteworthy phrase was added, "It is not the responsibility of the Allied Powers to impose upon Japan any form of government not supported by the freely expressed will of the people."[5]

Thus the stage was set for the occupation. Meanwhile, the Japanese refused to give up, especially under unconditional terms. Japanese leaders wouldn't have dared to mention such dishonorable, un–Japanese terms like "surrender." They had been trained to accept death as an honor rather than ever surrender and disgrace the nation. They were willing to continue the war even on their home ground, in 1945. But the atomic bomb settled that.

Two Bureaucracies Implement Policy

The decision to use the existing form of government in Japan was made because American officials were initially dependent on the Japanese for information. The Japanese people were to obey the instructions issued from their own government leaders. Although this did not hinder the implementation of Allied policy, it did cause confusion, because it led to the operation of two different bureaucracies.

From the Japanese point of view, the Occupation marked an entirely new stage in their history. The Meiji had produced a strong, centralized nation-state and provided an industrial base for its expanding economy. The leaders planned and the people followed.

Then, almost overnight, General MacArthur virtually became the dictator of Japan. The Far Eastern Commission and the Allied Council of Japan, both legal international bodies established by the Council of Foreign Ministers in Moscow, had no real power. Under General MacArthur and his Far Eastern Command, an elaborate bureaucracy developed in Tokyo. The organization included more than 3000 military officers and civilians, appropriately divided into staff sections. The names of the sections indicated the scope of their responsibilities: Diplomatic, Economic and Scientific, Legal, Public Health and Welfare, Natural Resources, Government, Civil Information and Education, Civil Transport, and Civil Communications. They corresponded to parallel functions or organizations in the Japanese government. The victorious powers chose not to depose the emperor nor destroy the framework of government, but rather to work through the existing structure in a manner reminiscent of the ancient Bakufu, the military bureaucracy that ruled Japan for nearly 700 years.

During World War II, the American government had undertaken a project to train American citizens, both civilians and soldiers, to administer the eventual occupation of Japan. There were about 200 high-ranking American army officers in the Japanese language and area training program set up at Stanford University alone. However, General MacArthur decided to use his own military staff instead of these specially trained persons. It was the beginning of his troubles with Washington.

The Japanese bureaucrats carried on their responsibilities, often reluctantly, and they received their instructions or directives on how to do so either orally or in writing from their counterparts in the Supreme Command for the Allied Powers (SCAP).

The basic objectives coincided to a great extent with the Potsdam agreement—1) limitation of Japan's sovereignty to its four main islands; 2) complete disarmament and demilitarization, plus the total annihilation of military influence; 3) encouraging the Japanese people to develop a desire for individual liberties and respect for fundamental human rights, and by doing so, establishing a form of democratic and representative government; and 4) providing an opportunity for the people to develop for themselves an economy which would permit the peaceful requirements of the population to be met.

Demilitarization, Democratization

The occupation of Japan took place in two basic stages. The first was to concentrate on demilitarization, democratization, and decentralization of the zaibatsu-dominated economy.

The first, demilitarization, was the easiest to accomplish. The cutting off of Japan's overseas possessions greatly reduced her military power. During the Occupation, both the army and navy were destroyed. Arsenals and factories engaged in producing military weapons were closed at once by the Occupation forces. All naval bases were destroyed and over two million officers and men in Japan were demobilized. In December 1945, the Army and Navy Ministries were transformed into the

First and Second Demobilization Ministries. The Potsdam Declaration had also stated, "There must be eliminated for all time the authority and influence of those who have deceived and misled the people of Japan into embarking on world conquest."

One important step in limiting the war-making possibilities was that major leaders of the aggression policy be punished as war criminals, as also specified by the Potsdam Declaration.

At the end of the war, more than 6.5 million Japanese soldiers and civilians were scattered throughout Asia and the Pacific islands. SCAP undertook the tremendous task of bringing them home and repatriated more than five million within a year. China, Korea, Vietnam, and the Philippines were glad to see the last of the Japanese, but their departure also caused an irreparable economic loss.

SCAP set up in Tokyo an international tribunal for the Far East "to mete out stern justice to all war criminals including those who have visited cruelties upon prisoners."

It began in January 1946, and during the next few years, some 2000 Japanese were banned from public life, and in some cases from important occupations. The policy toward those men gave no credence to the idea of possible reeducation. Rather, those individuals who were found guilty were outlawed on a permanent basis. An international war crimes tribunal was set up in Tokyo to try the war leaders including the wartime prime minister, General Tojo, and a number of others including Generals Doihara and Itagaki, the chief architects of Japan's continental policies; General Matsui, commander of the Japanese forces during the rape of Nanking; and Hirota, the former prime minister and civilian front man for the army. They were held personally responsible for conspiring to wage aggressive war and committing crimes against peace. They were hanged. Over 5000 other Japanese war leaders were given prison terms of varying lengths. Their punishment satisfied the sense of justice on the part of the victorious, but brought little consolation to the losers. The Japanese doubted the justice of heaping the guilt of the nation on the shoulders of its leaders.

The emperor was not subjected to trial, nor was Prince Higashikuni, who had condemned the captured Doolittle flyers to beheading. As for the American policy during these trials, it was the general belief that guilt must be established and the guilty punished as an obligation to our own war dead and as a reminder to would-be aggressors of the future.

The demilitarization process was relatively easy compared to the democratization of occupied Japan. SCAP assumed some of the characteristics of a missionary that first year, an evangelical and paternal enterprise of dynamic reform. More than 1000 directives from SCAP to the Japanese government ordered the remaking of Japan. General MacArthur set the tone and determined the tempo of a frantic, yet deliberate, process of cultural diffusion. Every office in Tokyo, every man in the street, and even the little people on the highways and byways of rural Japan were made conscious of the nationwide drive for democratization or Americanization.

General MacArthur himself remained almost completely aloof from the Japanese people. He seldom ventured from the beaten path between his residence at the American embassy and SCAP headquarters. If anyone wanted to see him, including the emperor, they had to call on him.

The Japanese were convinced of superior American military power, but they were skeptical of the values of the American way of life. Some even thought that their emperor would discover a new mission and regain international prestige for Japan which the blundering generals and admirals had lost.

The irony was that SCAP itself was an autocratic military organization that exhibited a certain amount of naivete about the practical workings of a democratic government. Can an authoritarian government ever teach democratic principles?

Japanese exponents of militarism and militant nationalism were removed and excluded from public office and all positions of public or substantial private responsibility. Ultranationalistic organizations like the Black Dragon society and the Reserve Officers' Association were dissolved. The program also removed 120,000 teachers (one out of every four) and about 200,000 others who had served in the armed services, the Imperial Rule Assistance Association, which was the only political party in 1940, the secret police, other militaristic societies, and the economic oligarchy. The purge did much to eliminate the old leadership group temporarily, but it compounded Japan's difficulties in the absence of a new leadership.

New Constitution

In the process of democratization, there were several areas of significant change in the political environment. First of all, the government section of SCAP drafted a new constitution that went into effect in May 1947 and on paper, it appeared as a most progressive political document. It placed sovereignty in the hands of the people, not the emperor, and took from the emperor most of his former prerogatives. It guaranteed civil liberties unconditionally, including the right to work, to bargain collectively, to be protected against economic exploitation, and to enjoy complete social equality. It provided for the separation of church and state, more local autonomy in government, and an independent judiciary with the right of judicial review.

Article 9 contained the revolutionary provision by which the Japanese people forever renounced war as a sovereign right and the threat or use of force as a means of settling international disputes, and pledged themselves never to maintain land, sea, air forces, or other war potential.

The new constitution also changed the nature and role of the emperor. The emperor had long been the figurehead of the Japanese state, believed to have been a descendant of a deity. Therefore, taking a position of hostility toward the emperor for allowing the aggression of Japan would have done little but antagonize the Japanese people and make the possibilities of constructive occupation more difficult. So the emperor became the tool that the Occupation used in establishing its policies. The major change in the power and position of the emperor was that he was forced to help pave the way for democracy by denouncing the myth that he was directed by a deity to rule the Japanese people. The emperor denounced his divinity on January 1, 1946, while the constitution of 1947 declared him to be a mere symbol of the state, so deriving his position from the will of the people in whom resides the sovereign power.[6] The decision to use the emperor on behalf of democracy and to shift the imperial institution into a kind of symbol, such as is represented by the British monarchy, was undoubtedly the most important decision made in the early period of the Occupation. The emperor adopted a program designed to humanize his position. He moved freely among the people and welcomed the people's cheers instead of bowing or hiding from them. He even took his wife to the ball game.

Such actions of the emperor naturally disturbed many conservative Japanese. They did not believe that the emperor's actions were voluntary. The abolition of state Shintoism and the humanizing of the emperor clashed head-on with the ideological base used by the militarists. Many Japanese refused to accept this Western approach.

The disappearance of the emperor myth necessitated a corresponding growth of ordinary democratic processes. These were difficult to produce. The former Prime Minister Yoshida stated in his memoirs that the Constitution of 1947 brought a new concept of the people's sovereignty, the emperor as a symbol, the establishment of a new Diet, individual liberties and rights, and a form of democratic government, rather than one of aristocratic nature.[7] Another historical change that the new constitution brought to the Japanese people was women's suffrage, a first in that nation's history.

One major aspect of the political reform established by the constitution was the decentralization and separation of the judiciary from the executive branch of government. A Supreme Court was formulated to function much like the judiciary branch of the United States.

In April, 1946, the first election took place. Prewar political parties of Minseito and Seiyukai won the majority. The Minseito party was closely associated with Mitsubishi zaibatsu interest while the Seiyukai party was associated with the Mitsui zaibatsu. The Minseito party leaned more toward the support of a general international trade and a sound money policy while the Seiyukai party supported Mitsui's mercantilism and continental expansionism.

Yoshida Shigern, formerly an associate of Baron Tanaka, a militarist, emerged as the establishment's political leader. He was acceptable to the Americans because he had had the good fortune of being thrown in jail by the militarists in 1945 for advocating an early end to the war. He served as prime minister during the first phase of the Occupation's reform movement.

In 1947, a new election was held. The Social-Democrats won the largest bloc of votes and named a Christian, Katayama Tetsu, as prime minister. That government lasted for only six months. In February 1948, the leader of the Democratic party, Ashida, took over but his government, too, ended after six months. Yoshida's conservative government returned and stayed in power until the end of the occupation.

The Japanese government's main responsibility was to carry out SCAP's orders, and Prime Minister Yoshida got along with General MacArthur better than Katayama and Ashida.

Constitutional change was the broad framework for political democratization, but many additional measures were taken. Rather extensive political decentralization was attempted with local and prefectural government bolstered in its powers and responsibilities. The traditional Japanese family system was sharply attacked in a variety of ways, and equality for women was written into the new Japanese laws. Major changes in the educational system were ordered. A land reform program conformed in general to the American idea of the family-owned farm. In the so-called economic decentralization program, another American idea was pursued—the reduction of monopoly and encouragement of competition.

Japanese Receptivity

The whole reform effort in Japan was fundamentally a long-range educational program. The American Occupation had to teach the Japanese people new attitudes and values as well as new techniques. Democracy depends as much on independence of judgment as on sound electoral procedures and broad parliamentary experience. The Japanese were a literate, newspaper-reading, radio-listening people. Thus, it was easy for the United States to bring new information and new ideas to them. At the end of the war, they were very receptive to new ideas because the totality of their defeat had destroyed any old concepts or beliefs they might have had before. Since it was so easy to communicate with the Japanese, and since they were so receptive to new ideas, it was quite easy to convince the vast majority that they had been misled by their war rulers and had been following an unsound course in pursuing an empire. The United States greatly influenced their thinking on a number of specific matters and implanted other ideas which had a profound influence in shaping the future of Japan.[8]

At the same time, America's greatest single mistake in

Japan was perhaps its failure to exploit this situation as fully as possible. Several factors held America back. One was the essential conflict in motives between the United States' desire to carry through a specific and immediate reform program and their long-term interest in fostering independence on the part of the Japanese public. One of the United States' major objectives in the educational field was to improve methods of spreading knowledge, in formal education as well as in other ways, so that the Japanese people might be better able to exercise these new-found freedoms, on which democracy depends. At the same time, the United States attempted to improve the school system and the curriculum.

Along with educational and political reforms, social reform had also to be initiated. This reform reached down to the family and relations between the sexes and age groups.

One of the most important aspects of the social reform was the attempt to readjust the balance of power between different economic and social groups by improving the economic status and stimulating the political development of certain classes. This could have shaken up the basic structure of Japanese society. But MacArthur's policy could not have afforded such a transformation in Japan. The United States government was committed to a policy that would help the Japanese become economically independent. The real question was, however, could the United States afford to let Japan become a free and independent state?

Economic Reform

Extensive economic reform was necessary to wrest economic power from the powerful zaibatsu group. MacArthur's military government needed to strengthen three classes of Japanese people who were to form the backbone of the new democracy—the working class, poor farmers, and small businessmen.

Traditionally, almost three-fourths of the farmers did not own their land. They paid rent up to half or more of their annual crops. Under the circumstances, it was imperative to institute land reform.

There were three general aims of the land reform—(1) to make more peasants landowners; (2) to serve all farmers with improved seeds and tools; and finally, (3) to grant farmers the independence necessary for them to participate actively in the postwar democratic setup.

The Allied Powers, therefore, considered the agricultural problems as one of the major questions to be solved in order to help Japan build a strong economic base for democracy. How the agrarian problem was seen by the American officials can be realized by a quote from the then Prime Minister Yoshida:

> Viewed from the standpoint of the Allied Powers, the Japanese land system was not only feudalistic, but it also harmed the national economy while providing the militarists with one of their firmest bases of support. The agrarian half of the nation represented a reservoir of soldiers and cheap labor. Rural landlords impeded the democratization of Japan equally with the militarists, financiers, and the bureaucracy. To end this state of affairs by liberating the agricultural classes and raising their living standards was, therefore, regarded by the Occupation authorities as a vital step in bringing about the demilitarization and democratization of Japan.[9]

So legislation was enacted and in 1946, the agrarian reform law had reluctantly passed in the Diet. The United States' policy toward the agrarian problem may be seen in the various provisions of the law. The Americans in Occupation headquarters wrote the reform—all agricultural land belonging to landowners who did not reside on it which was being tilled solely by peasants, was to be transferred to the tenants. Individual ownership of tenant land was to be limited to one cho (2.45 acres—four cho in Hokkaido). The total amount of agricultural land that could be owned individually, including tenant land, was to be limited to three cho (twelve cho in Hokkaido). It was compulsory that any land held beyond that limit would be sold to the government for resale to tenant farmers, and payments to landowners for their requisitioned land was to be made in government bonds. The result of these land reform policies was a redistribution of two million cho of agricultural land to some 1.5 million landowners. The ancient pattern of land ownership changed rapidly as a result of the reforms. By 1949, land held by owner-farmers increased from 53.7 percent to 86.9 percent of the total arable land. The number of farmers who owned all their land increased from 36.3 percent to 61.6 percent by 1950.[10] The land reform resulted in important political phenomena which the Japanese government did not anticipate. Radical elements among the peasantry tended to disappear as they became increasingly interested in maintaining their new property and liberty gains. They strongly supported the conservative parties. We see, therefore, that the land reforms also served the political objectives of the American policy.

It must be realized, however, that redistribution of property could not possibly solve the problem of poverty and overpopulation on Japan's 14.7 million acres of arable land.

One of the more constructive economic policies during the first phase—1945–1947—of the Occupation was the breaking down of the all-powerful zaibatsu. The policy was based on the Allied Powers' agreed-on pledge which was to insure "a wide and just distribution of income and ownership of the means of production and trade."[11] Essentially this meant the dispersal of the zaibatsu hold on the nation's economy and redistribution of the wealth.

Zaibatsu Come Under Fire

The zaibatsu group, which gained tremendous amounts of economic power during the Meiji rule, had become strongly favored by the government and was the group of people that supplied Japan with the needed industries for fighting a war. The zaibatsu, the financial-military-industrial-monopolistic clique, literally controlled the economy in all aspects. The concentration of Japan's industrial and commercial wealth and power gave the Occupation a major headache. These were the few very, very rich families known as the zaibatsu. This zaibatsu system, a major factor in Japan's aggressive war policies, could not be separated from Japanese militarism.

Mitsui, the largest zaibatsu, and Sumitomo, the third largest, dated back to the seventeenth century. The zaibatsu system is unique to Japan. Not all are involved in the same business, but most are engaged in various kinds of businesses to be discussed later. Mitsui, Mitsubishi, and Sumitomo had been involved in commerce, banking, as well as both light and heavy industries. Yasuda, Kawasaki, and Shibuzawa concentrated more on finance and banking, and Asano and Okura on industry. These enormous houses with great economic power had been dominating the politics as well as the business of Japan. Some were organized strictly as family trusts, and others reached out to outside alliances, in which strong feudalistic loyalties were practiced. But whether the relationship was based on a holding company and a subsidiary, or between the employer and the employee, there were clear obligations among them. Sometimes there were written contracts but mostly they were unwritten ones. Regardless of the many changes that have taken place in the structure and communication of Japanese business, the zaibatsu are still the most dominant factor in Japan today.

On April 20, 1946, the Holding Company Liquidation Commission was created. In June, twenty-nine zaibatsu holding companies were ordered to make available complete records of their assets and liabilities. They were forbidden to make new investments and their bank accounts and the activities of their executives were frozen. The operating and subsidiary shares of the five largest companies were taken over by the government in September and made available for sale to the public. Private ownership of capital was discouraged with a levy starting at 25 percent for individuals holding over 100,000 yen and up to 90 percent for those holding over 15 million yen.[12] Members of zaibatsu families and the executives of their concerns were cut off from connections with business enterprises and excluded from holding public office.

The high officials of four main zaibatsu groups: Mitsui, Mitsubishi, Sumitomo, and Yasuda (which manipulated almost the entire economy of Japan), were ordered to resign and to cease influencing the management of their companies. Their properties were to be sold to outsiders. To some Americans, this seemed socialistic. Naturally, this policy drew much criticism, not only among the Japanese, but also from the Americans. SCAP defended its policies and intentions as the first step necessary in establishing a system of free, private, competitive enterprise and as indispensible to the growth of democratic government.

The dissolution of the holdings of vast wealth and family fortunes brought an end to the great Japanese combines by eliminating their central organs, and laws were passed to prevent their recreation. The Diet passed two laws, the Anti-Monopoly Law of 1947 and the Trade Association Law of 1948. These were designed to carry out the occupational directives and to prevent the reappearance of monopolistic companies and practices. The laws were difficult to enforce and were honored as much in the breach as in the observance. The occupation authorities decided, nevertheless, to break up corporations they considered excessive concentrations of economic power.

Startling Rearmament of Japan

Demilitarization, decentralization, and democratization again were the stated tasks assigned to the Occupation forces. SCAP had attempted to fulfill its responsibility by carrying them out with considerable enthusiasm during the first phase. Even during the early stage of the second phase, SCAP had insisted on decentralization of the zaibatsu. Then, all of a sudden, in 1947 General MacArthur changed his policy completely by giving up the entire program of the first phase, and instead initiated a rearmament program, a direct contradiction of the original policy.

Why did General MacArthur change and pave the way for a resurgence of Japanese militarism? Two basic realities influenced MacArthur. The first was the domestic condition of Japan, and the second was international, in particular the political situation in Asia, which had changed a great deal since early 1949.

A new democratic political, social system had been introduced earlier, but it had hardly destroyed the basic economic structure. The fundamental changes in economic and political balance of power were never effected. The first phase of the Occupation had given some hope to the possible democratization of Japan but such wishful thinking began to fade as General MacArthur sensed danger from the Japanese left-wing radical movement.

The war not only had brought the material destruction of Japan, but had also created doubts about the ruling class and their ability as national leaders. As a matter of fact, both internal and external conditions existed to create a revolutionary change in Japan.

American policy in Japan maintained that the basic capitalistic system must be saved, and the American government decided to recover and support the traditional economic system of Japan in 1949. To back up this policy, a strong sovereign nation needed a sufficient military force. General MacArthur and his military associates also believed that rebuilding Japanese economic and military power would provide a safeguard against the growing Communist movement in Asia.

Consequently, the first phase of demilitarization, democratization, decentralization had to be changed. And it was no easy task to take away freedom from the people, once they had learned to enjoy it. The democracy that the Allied Powers had introduced in Japan was a bourgeois democracy. It contained, nevertheless, some of the first basic freedoms that nation had ever experienced. Trade unions had been legalized, poor tenant farmers owned a piece of land for the first time, the extreme militarists and their collaborators like Hirota had been punished, and many ultranationalistic organizations like the Black Dragon Society had been disbanded. Democratization of the police force and the women's suffrage had also been effected. On the whole, individual rights had been respected and peace became the basic concept of Japan's new constitution. All these progressive changes had been suddenly threatened by the swift change in the Occupation policy.

The changed policy not only meant the reverse of earlier democratic policy, but it was a betrayal of the Potsdam commitment.

MacArthur Fears Liberal Power

Even though the working class and the poor farmers had gained democratic freedoms in the early stages of Occupation, they were soon confronted with an economic crisis, inflation that endangered their newly gained rights. In spite of this, MacArthur's policy was to support the ruling class by suppressing the working class and the poor farmers. His fear of left-wing radical growth in Japan was a genuine concern. He was obviously alarmed by the fact that conservative political power was decreasing, especially in the urban areas, while progressive and liberal political sentiment had gained greater influence among urban youth, organized labor, and the intellectuals. It was only the rural people who still gave the conservatives support. General MacArthur had to reassess his occupational policy, with advice from Washington.

What were the external conditions that influenced the American Occupation policy? After 1946, the United States had gradually become aware of the fact that its original premises concerning Asia were no longer valid. America had supported and counted on a Nationalistic China to serve as the great stabilizer and democratic symbol of Asia. But the signs for Nationalist China became increasingly unfavorable. All of Asia was in a kind of power vacuum produced by the precipitous withdrawal of Western powers on the one hand, and the weakness of the newly independent or reorganized Asian governments on the other. Political and economic unrest in the Far East and the nationalistic movements of South and Southeast Asia were reaching a peak, with the old colonial powers as their main targets. The United States viewed the situation as critical. This was all the more important because American relations with the Soviet Union had deteriorated, and because the United States then strongly believed that the Soviet-led forces of world Communism would use any tactics to fill the power vacuum of Asia, building on their footholds in China, North Korea, and other regions. Thus, the era of the cold war and containment of Communism had begun and also affected American policy toward Japan.

Dodge Plan

Thus in Japan, a new word, called "recovery," was coined. This recovery led to a Nine-Point Stabilization Program at the end of 1948. By utilizing this program, the United States sought to restore stability to the Japanese economy by such measures as a balanced budget, improved tax collection, credit restrictions, wage and price controls, trade expansion, production increases, and improved food collection. The so-called Dodge Plan achieved considerable success, and 1949 represented a year of relative price stability and acceleration of recovery in many areas of the Japanese economy. It was called the Dodge Plan because of the work of Joseph M. Dodge, a Detroit banker, appointed by President Truman as General MacArthur's financial adviser. This same man had played an important part in the German currency reform. Therefore, he went to Japan with impressive credentials. With his instant grasp of the underlying problems, and sure handling of both material and human aspects, Mr. Dodge contributed greatly to the recovery program's success. American efforts extended to areas of Japanese foreign influence as well as domestic. Both reparations and trade policies were involved.

The United States, at first, had favored heavy reparations as some measure of repayment for damages and as an insurance against future Japanese ascendancy. The Pauley Report on Japanese Reparations issued in 1948 was a clear expression of this point of view. But the so-called Johnston Committee Report that followed shortly took a less drastic position, scaling down earlier recommendations for the dismantlement of heavy industry. American policy moved toward what could be called a viewpoint that any large reparations to countries claiming compensation for Japanese wartime damage would have to be paid directly or indirectly by the United States. At the same time, Japanese trade began to take on a new vigor. A large percentage of trade was now conducted with the United States as a natural result of American credits and the drastic reduction of the northeast Asian market for Japan. In addition, Japan now began to seek markets in Southeast Asia with American encouragement. Consequently, Japan became the chief foreign investor in Thailand, Taiwan, South Korea, Indonesia, and other parts of Asia. This aggressive economic movement of Japan had been urged by the United States. Japan was also protected by the United States, who was playing the role of middle man between Japan and the outside world. This economic recovery took priority in the minds of MacArthur and his associates and wherever reform measures seemed to threaten recovery, they did not hesitate to restructure or abandon altogether. Naturally, the economic decentralization program of the zaibatsu system had been completely abandoned.

Japan, Western Watchdog

Once General MacArthur and policy-makers in Washington decided to restore Japan as a power in order to play a major role in Asia, MacArthur became impatient with the slow response from Japanese leaders. They were not at all sure what MacArthur was up to. To a defeated people, war had become unpopular, and militarism was condemned by the majority of people. No leader dared suggest restoring militarism at that time, even though MacArthur wanted to fill the power gap in the Far East with Japan. The primary aim of the occupation was to build a democratic Japan, not necessarily overnight, but rather over a long period of time. Having changed the closed society to an open one, the democratic forces of Japan were free to participate in the process of decision-making.

For instance, in their new election in 1947, the Socialist party became the largest single party, an event that MacArthur had not anticipated. It showed how little the General and his American associates understood the national mood of Japan at the time.

Prime Minister Katayama, a socialist, organized the first socialist government in the history of Japan. How could a Socialist government get along with General MacArthur? Even conservatives like Shidehara and Yoshida had at first failed to get along with the General; therefore, there was no hope at all for the Socialists. The Socialist government resigned, to be replaced by a coalition government. The coalition became unpopular and another election took place. The 1949 election resulted in a conservative majority. Yoshida, the leader of the conservative Liberal-Democratic party, formed a new government. With his previous experience, Yoshida was ready to deal with MacArthur.

As early as March 1947, MacArthur thought that the Japanese were ready for a peace treaty. What that really meant was that Japan could play a new role as a watchdog in Asia as she had done before in the first half of the century. Only this time the master of the dog would be the United States, not the British Empire.

The problem arose among the Far East Commission (FEC) members as to how the drafting of the treaty for Japan should proceed. All this dragged on for almost two years due to disagreement between the United States, China, and the Soviet Union on essential questions. General MacArthur reaffirmed his view over and over that the Japanese had done all they could and had in fact fulfilled their obligations to the

Potsdam Declaration. He stated directly to the Japanese people themselves that they were not at fault and to be patient. The treaty dealt with the restoration of prewar property rights in Japan and the settlement of property claims. The security problem, and the question of Soviet and Chinese participation, was not to be completely resolved until after 1949.

MacArthur paid little attention to other members of the Far East Commission. Japan was his personal kingdom.

At the beginning of 1950, General MacArthur believed that Japan was an oasis of tranquility and progress and that "no place on earth was more completely at peace." With this statement, the General initiated Japanese military power again in the postwar period by approving 75,000 men to make up a national police force. This number soon rose to 100,000 and included former officers of the Japanese army. The name was changed to National Security Force, and tanks were included in its arsenal of weapons. After the signing of the peace treaty, a Self-Defense Air Force and naval force were created. These forces have been increasing steadily ever since.

In January 1951, the United States drafted the principles of the peace settlement with Japan. This draft was then circulated among more than twenty nations.

As a result of its own deliberations, the United Kingdom drafted a text based upon the results of the Commonwealth conferences. In June, the United States and the United Kingdom pooled their efforts and drafted a third text. This new text was circulated during the first two weeks of July and kept open for further changes until the middle of August, 1951.

The role of the Soviet Union during all this preliminary work was active but unfavorable. Secretary of State John Foster Dulles had conferred with Soviet delegate Malik several times, and their respective governments exchanged some ten memoranda and drafts. Despite continued hostilities, the Soviet Union accepted the invitation extended by the United States and the United Kingdom as cosponsors to attend a conference at the San Francisco Opera House to conclude a treaty of peace with Japan. They accepted because they believed they could improve some of the contents of the treaty. Foreign Minister Gromyko's effort to change the content failed, and he walked out.

The principal provisions of the treaty included: 1) territory—reduced to four main islands; 2) security—Japan accepted the charter of the United Nations; 3) reparations—"It is recognized that Japan should pay reparations to the Allied powers for the damage and suffering" it caused during the war.

As the treaty reveals, Japan got off with a light sentence. The United States government wanted to make sure that Japan's interests would be protected. Japan's interests coincided with America's; at least, that's what the decision-makers in Washington believed, ironic as it may seem today.

As long as the conservatives, supported by the zaibatsu, controlled the Japanese government, the relationship between Japanese and American interests would probably dovetail. But there is no such guarantee of political monopoly in Japan today in spite of the conservatives' two-thirds majority in both houses of the Diet. It is already too late to curtail the democratic movement which the Allied Powers initiated during their early stage Occupation.

Organized trade union members number almost eleven million. The Socialist party, supported by most of Japan's urban intellectuals, and the mass media that dominate public opinion, are all important evidence of democratic forces in Japan today.

Notes

1. Philip W. Taylor, "The Administration of Occupied Japan," *The Annals,* Vol. 267 (Philadelphia: The American Academy of Political and Social Science, 1950), pp. 140–153.

2. Francis Miller, *War in Korea and Complete History of World War II* (New York: Holt, Rinehart, Winston, 1952), p. 24.

3. Ibid, p. 41.

4. Lawrence Rosinger, "The Occupation of Japan," *Foreign Policy Reports,* May 15, 1947, p. 52.

5. Ibid.

6. Kazuo Kawai, *Japan's American Interlude* (Chicago: University of Chicago Press, 1960), p. 71.

7. Shigeru Yoshida, *The Yoshida Memoirs* (Boston: Houghton Mifflin, 1962), p. 126.

8. E. O. Reischauer, *The United States and Japan* (Cambridge, Mass.: Harvard University Press, 1957), p. 263.

9. Yoshida, *Memoirs,* p. 196.

10. Ibid, p. 201.

11. John C. Campbell, *The U.S. in World Affairs* (New York: Harper, 1948), p. 150.

12. Reischauer, *United States and Japan,* p. 275.

7 Revival of Japanese Militarism

The infamous Japanese slogan of its New Order in East Asia was a precipitating factor in World War II. By the same token, the restoration of Japan as a military power in Asia will once again threaten peace in Asia—not necessarily against China or Russia, as American decision-makers planned, but against America itself. Very simply, the crucial conflict of economic interest is not between Japan and China or Russia, *but between Japan and the United States.*

During the decade 1931–1941, the balance of power in Japan moved toward the militarists and the New Order was their invention. Japanese militarists were traditionally anti-Western, anticapitalist, and advocated national socialism or fascism in Japanese style. The militarists were adventurers. They preferred war and the risk of defeat rather than remaining subject to foreign influence and domination. The Japanese economy is under the influence and domination of giant American corporations today, and the Japanese militarists cannot accept the present arrangement. Either conceptually or practically, such an arrangement is alien to the "purity-minded" Japanese military tradition. The militarists had believed their mission to be that of liberating nonwhite peoples from Anglo-Saxon domination, and strengthening their government to secure "Asia for the Asiatics." The slogan of "Asia for Asiatics" was completely false. That concept of the Nixon doctrine that suggests that indigenous people should defend their security while America aids them with material supplies is similarly false. "Asia for Asiatics" meant Asia for the Japanese. Asians were not fooled by Japanese or American propaganda.

Containment Policy in Asia

The concept of the Truman–Dulles containment policy and the Nixon doctrine indicates that America has much to learn about Japan. The Japanese militarists had said they wished to emancipate Asia from Communist control. When Japan invaded Manchuria, Chinese territory, in the name of anticommunism, not only the United States and Great Britain, but also Chiang Kai-shek himself remained neutral. There had been active Korean Communist guerrilla movements on the borders of Korea and Manchuria and Japan claimed as her legitimate right the sending of imperial troops to Chinese territory in order to suppress Communist movement. Chiang Kai-shek accepted it. But Mao Tse-tung did not. Any nation that receives American aid because it is "invaded" by indigenous Communists is no different than Manchuria was in 1931.

Japanese militarists said that the purpose of their invasion of China was to purge China of Communism as Japan had purged itself of Westernization. They did not discriminate; they were against both capitalism and Communism as ideologies of Western origin. They thought that they had found a justification for the New Order in anti-Western attitudes. Today, the militarists once again seek a justification to restore their traditional concept of superiority.

There are many contradictions in such a movement today. First of all, Japanese militarism can only be restored when Japanese capitalists decide to do so. And the Japanese capitalists can do this only when the American capitalists allow them to. In spite of the sharp conflict of economic interests (as they appear today between the two nations), American corporations have decided to support the restoration of Japanese militarism.

The struggle for markets, the control of major industries, and the role of capital finance are all mixed up in this vital issue.

That is why both Japanese and American governments are trying, in desperation, to find ways to rationalize the conflict. It is not a matter of one industry dominating another; rather it is a matter of the entire economic and social relationships between the two nations. The contradiction is no different than it was with the anti-Comintern Pact of 1936. Japan joined Germany and Italy to fight against the Soviet Union because they all believed then the Soviet Union was their common enemy. Japanese militarists claimed that they were anti-Western, but joined Germany and Italy for their own interest. For her own interests, that is, militarism, there is absolutely no assurance that America can trust Japan and vice versa. The contradiction has existed not only among the powers, but has existed also between ruling groups in Japan. Zaibatsu interests and the military interests have not always coincided. The extreme militarists often pursued their aggressive policies against the policies of their own government. The Manchurian Incident was one such case.

Rise of Militarism

Another contradiction in the restoration of Japanese militarism is the matter of international trade. Japan will pursue her present aggressive export policy even though she frequently confronts her American partner in the future. It was the United States that elevated the Japanese economy to the position it has now, and it will be Japan who will challenge the United States.

For example, Japan has increasingly engaged in weapons manufacturing supported by American investment. This is a clear violation of her constitution as well as the spirit of the San Francisco Peace Treaty. Table 3 shows how Japan has busily engaged in weapons exports.

What companies are manufacturing such weapons? To what extent are these companies associated with American corporations? Who makes a profit out of the weapons business? Do or have these business programs coincided with the Vietnam War? Clearly, there are answers to these questions. The

Table 3

Weapons Export by Japan[1]

Date	Export to	Kinds of Weapons	Amount*
1966	Thailand	Rifles, 5000	19,330
	U.S.A.	Variety of Guns	4576
	South Korea	Shells	45
1967	U.S.A.	Guns, Swords, etc.	7488
	Taiwan	Shells, Gun Powder	1626
	England	Variety of Guns	51
	France	Variety of Guns	43
1968	U.S.A.	Guns and other firearms	8565
	South Korea	Shells	268
	France	Guns	77
	Hong Kong	Guns	58
	Australia	Rifles	47
1969+	U.S.A.	Guns	2936
	Philippines	Guns, Gun Powder	1450
	Canada	Rifles	31

*10,000-yen unit
+1st 6 months

leading Japanese companies are the major producers of the weapons, and closely related to the American companies.

Table 4 indicates who dominated the weaponry business in Japan in 1968. It also tells which company produces what kind of weapon.

Table 4

Ten Leading Companies Dominate War Machineries in Japan (1968)[2]

Company	Amount*	Type of Goods
Mitsubushi Heavy Industry	394.1	Airplanes, weapons of all kinds, ships, parts, etc.
Mitsubushi Electric	330.8	Weapons, Communication equipment
Tokyo Shibaura Electric	120.0	Electric equipment
Nippon Airplane Manufacturer	91.2	Airplanes
Nippon Steel	88.1	Weapons
Ishigawajima-Harima	80.7	Airplane engines
Kawajaki Airplane	77.4	Airplanes and repairings
Nippon Electric	68.7	Weapons, Communication equipment
Meiwa Industries	31.4	Airplanes and repairings
Komatsu Manufacturing	27.7	Weapons, others
Total	1310.1	

*10,000-yen unit

The total amount consisted of about 60 percent of the entire budget of the office of national defense of Japan in 1968. In other words, the ten leading companies headed by the Mitsubishi zaibatsu group control 60 percent of the national defense business in Japan. Mitsubishi Heavy Industries has a very close association with Lockheed, Douglas, North America Aviation, and Sikorsky of the United States; Tokyo Shibaura Electric has a similar association with Litton Industries; Ishikawajima-Harima is allied with General Electric, Kawajaki Airplane has a close contact with Bell, Boeing, and Lockheed; and Meiwa Heavy Industry has a close contact with Grumman.

Japan's Overseas Investment

In other words, none of these Japanese war industries can survive without American financial and technical aid. The ties between Japanese and American war industries are increasing instead of declining. Why does Japan attract American investment when she needs to export her own surplus capital? This is another contradiction of the relationship with Americans. Japanese overseas capital investment amounted to $231 million in 1967, and increased to $514 million the following year, and continues its acceleration. Japanese investment abroad has been activated with the enthusiasm of their American counterpart, and the weapons race has begun again.

Table 5 shows the geographic areas of Japanese economic concentration. Indicative of the economic-military-technological relationships between the two nations about which the general public is unaware is the fact that the United States has invested more in Japan than in Vietnam for American defense. At the time of the escalation of war in Vietnam in 1964–1965, the United States had invested $321 million in Japan as compared with $64 million in Vietnam. In 1965, the amount increased to $346 million in Japan and $188 million in Vietnam. Even in 1969, the amount ran up to $320 million in Japan, while it was $303 million in Vietnam.[3] The war was in Vietnam, but the United States invested more money in Japan. Why? Because the United States government wanted to build up Japan as her Asian partner in spite of the future threat of Japanese competition.

Table 5

Japanese Capital Investment Abroad (in millions of dollars)[4]

	North America	Latin America	Southeast Asia	Europe	Others
1967	$ 57	$ 41	$ 54	$ 30	$ 49
1968	186	41	72	151	64
Total to 1968	$594	$414	$355	$210	$360

Japanese competition with American interests in Asian countries is clearly indicated in her aid and exports to various Asian nations where once the United States dominated. In South Korea, for instance, 93.6 percent of foreign aid came from the United States in 1965, but the situation had changed in 1968. Japanese aid to South Korea accounted for 31.7 percent of the total while the United States' share was reduced to 44.9 percent. In 1965, American aid to Taiwan amounted to 74.9 percent of all foreign aid while Japan accounted for only 19.9 percent. But in 1968, American aid declined to 24.8 percent while Japanese aid increased to 55.2 percent of the total.

Table 6, a comparison of aid and exports of Japan and America in Asian countries, gives a clear picture of this trend.

Table 6

Comparative Situation of Aid and Exports by Japan and America in Asian Countries (% base)[5]

	To South Korea		To Taiwan		To Philippines	
	1965	1968	1965	1968	1965	1968
Japanese Aid	....	31.7%	19.9%	55.2%	....	44.6%
American Aid	93.6%	44.9	74.9	24.8	....	20.7
	1966					
Japanese Export	46.8	41.0	40.0	41.0	28.3	33.4
American Export	35.4	24.4	22.0	27.0	45.4	45.2

More impressive figures are shown in Table 7. In 1961, there were only $96.3 million of Japanese goods exported to Taiwan, but the amount increased to $663.6 million by 1969. Similar increases have been shown in other countries—South Korea, South Vietnam, Thailand, Malaysia, the Philippines, and Hong Kong.

Table 7

Japanese Exports to Southeast Asia[6] (in $ millions)

	1961	1969
Taiwan	$ 96.32	$663.60
South Korea	125.88	767.19
Hong Kong	153.53	614.57
South Vietnam	65.71	223.16
Thailand	133.87	443.84
Malaysia	31.78	133.45
Philippines	118.18	475.61
Total	$725 million	$3.3 billion

Exports in Asia

Japanese world trade amounted to $1.4 billion in 1961, and $4.4 billion in 1969. In other words, almost three-fourths of total Japanese exports were concentrated in Southeast Asian countries in 1969. Comparing this with Japanese imports from the same area is also revealing. In 1961, the total imports of Japan amounted to $975 million from these countries and $2.4 billion in 1969. The interesting change is that the Japanese exports in 1961 were far less than her imports, but the situation reversed in 1969 in favor of Japan. All these favorable situations have been created as part of American policy to build up Japan as her watchdog in Asia.

Imperialism Under New Guise

Is Japanese imperialism a reality today? All evidence indicates that Japanese imperialism has indeed been restored. How can Japanese imperialism claim its independence and yet be subjugated to American imperialism at the same time? There is danger of confusion here.

First of all, Japanese imperialism is an independent reality; secondly and simultaneously, Japanese imperialism is also subjugated to American imperialism. This is a contradiction but the main reason for this phenomenon is that a new multinational corporate system is appearing in the world. Such an economic system is possible because the profit motive has no limits or boundaries; it is a supra-national system.

Under American leadership, the United Kingdom, West Germany, France, Italy, and now Japan, have become capitalistic although the struggle for national interest continues. Under the international capitalistic bloc, Japan is not free to exercise her own will, but must follow the collective will of the big powers. The situation becomes more obvious when it involves matters of diplomacy and military affairs. As long as this relationship exists, Japan will remain a junior partner of American capitalism. This situation, however, does not eliminate the increasingly severe competition between Japanese and American economic interests.

Japanese capital must expand in order to survive just as American capital must expand for its survival. That is the heart of American business. Japanese capital investments in South Korea, Taiwan, the Philippines, Indonesia, and elsewhere are a matter of economic survival.

Japanese overseas investment increased 100 percent during 1968–1970 compared to 1961–1967. The amount reached $1.2 billion in 1972, and $6.8 billion in the first three months of 1973. According to Nippon Kyogyo Bank, Japanese overseas investments will reach $42.5 billion by 1980, and about one-fourth of it will be invested in Southeast Asian countries including South Korea, Hong Kong, and Taiwan.[7] These investments, contrary to Japanese claims, do not support either modernization or industrialization nor is the standard of living of these nations raised. Japanese investment supports the privileged classes only. In 1973, according to figures released by the South Korean government, a cumulative total of $523 million in foreign investment has been accepted since 1962. A breakdown shows that Japan has invested $315 million, the United States, $171 million, and other countries, $37 million. What is alarming is the investment trend. In the first six months of 1973, Japan invested about $159 million while the second largest investor, the United States, invested only $2 million. Japan accounted for more than 90 percent of foreign investment in South Korea in 1973, but the Japanese are not in Korea to provide jobs for unemployed Korean workers. The return on capital invested and profits made by foreigners in Korea amounted to $16 million in the first half of 1973. The cumulative total since 1962 is over $52 million. The South Korean government advertised these figures in the *New York Times* to attract more American investors.[8] The creation of multinational corporations has been encouraged in Japan with what economists call "liberalization." Liberalization provides free opportunity for large capital investors—Americans are free to invest their capital in Japan while Japanese investors are free to do likewise in the United States. They agree that such freedom is economically essential to maximize their profits.

Is Japan a Military Threat?

Freedom to move capital across national boundaries implies that political stability is assured the investors. It is for this reason that the United States government consistently supports foreign dictatorships. They provide that necessary political stability. Foreign investors are fully aware of the dangers of national resistance, and the resulting insecurity of their capital investments. The investors, therefore, demand a high rate on their return. This requires intensive exploitation of the workers in many underdeveloped countries.

In the case of Japan, she is second only to the United States in growth of gross national products but twentieth in rank in 1973 as far as per capita income is concerned. Japanese wages are basically low, and the accumulation of capital is accelerating as a result. Why shouldn't American companies invest capital in Japan and other Asian countries? Not only do workers in Japan sacrifice their wages, but the workers in America lose jobs whenever American employers invest in Japan. The multi-national corporations are engaged in such a conspiracy against the wage-earners everywhere.

Japanese capitalism is playing a role in this international system of capitalism. The danger is clear. One day Japanese militarists, with the aid of their business partners, will decide to strike back at America or any other country in the name of "peace" in Asia or "Asian co-prosperity" or "Asia for Asiatics," with well-developed nuclear weapons; it will be too late to regret what America has done to rebuild Japanese military power.

Japan has today the fifth largest armed force in the world, and she is also capable of making sophisticated nuclear weapons, as her leaders have stated in public. All Japan needs is a delivery system, which she is certainly more than capable of making. Who can deny the danger of Japanese militarism today?

Notes

1. See *Tsukan Dokei* or *Customs Statistics,* 1970, 1971, Tokyo.

2. Compiled from *Asia Trend Year Book,* 1970; *The Present Condition and Problems of Economic Cooperation,* 1969; *Tsushow Hakushow* or *White Paper of Trade,* 1970, Tokyo.

3. *Present Condition and Problems of Economic Cooperation,* 1969, Tokyo.

4. Ibid.

5. *Asia Trend Year Book,* 1970, Tokyo.

6. Imagawa Eiichi, "The Japanese Economy's Rush into Asia," *Sekai,* (Tokyo, November 1970).

7. Jun Nishikawa, "The Economy of Southeast Asia," in *Sekai,* No. 343 (Tokyo, June 1974), p. 44.

8. *The New York Times,* Section 12, November 4, 1973, p. 15

8 Reemergence of Zaibatsu

American Occupation policy was reversed in 1949 in order to check Japanese left-wing radical movement that included both communists and socialists, by reenfranchising the conservative political and economic forces. In view of the rapid growth of the Japanese working class and poor farmers, and the existence of the Democratic People's Republic of Korea, such steps were deemed necessary by American policy-makers.

The Dodge economic plan initiated in 1949 was a significant step in reconstructing the zaibatsu system, a monopolistic bloc, that the Allied Powers had dispersed just a few years earlier. Coincidentally, the Korean war became an important factor in accelerating the reemergence of zaibatsu. The Japanese economy also began to recover almost immediately by supplying military goods to American soldiers in Korea.

The Japanese government, along with the Bank of Japan, supported by American capital and technical aid, reestablished the basic Japanese industries of electric power, coal, steel and iron, and shipping. Thus the foundation for the economic growth and development was established during the years of 1950–1954, the duration of the Korean war.

At the end of that war, the zaibatsu group emerged again with a concentration of capital when the rest of the economy faced difficulties. The major characteristic of the zaibatsu at this time was its dependence on American business support. The relationship between American and Japanese business was that of master and subordinate. For necessary raw materials, for markets for manufactured goods, and even for its food supply, Japan had to rely on the United States. Japan also needed to cultivate a new industry because of the decline in her textile exports. The world textile market had grown extremely competitive. Japanese zaibatsu began to develop chemical and electronic industries with American capital and technical aid. Such a symbiotic economic relationship created an inevitable political closeness. On September 8, 1951, forty-nine nations signed a peace treaty with Japan, but on that same day, the United States had concluded a separate security pact with Japan. Thus the American-Japanese National Defense Agreement went hand-in-hand with signing of the peace treaty.

Japan—Foil Against Communism

This, of course, was also the time of the Korean conflict. Not only did the United States want to build up Japan as her Asian partner, but Japan, too, wanted to take a stand on the Korean conflict. The Japanese stated clearly that in the conflict between Communism and the free world, she had no choice but to choose the free world. Such a commitment was important for the international scene and also made points at home.

The purposes of the peace treaty and the security pact were to rebuild Japan in order to balance the power against Communist China. The Japanese ruling class was more than willing to cooperate in the new assignment.

During 1955–1961, the Japanese economy established its high rate of growth. Such success was possible because of American aid, technical and otherwise. The old familiar zaibatsu group had been restored, and some new monopolies emerged.

Before analyzing the postwar zaibatsu group activities, the historical background of the zaibatsu should be explained briefly.

The Meiji Restoration leaders needed tremendous political power in order to push through the economic changes they had in mind. They had been determined from the first to construct an economy sufficiently industrialized to enable Japan to hold her own in the modern world.

Restoration leaders had forced through most of the measures necessary for the development of a capitalist economy even before they were compelled to grant Japan a constitution in 1889.

They compromised feudal institutions by legalizing the private property system in Western style. They established compulsory education, organized efficient departments of central and local government, and removed the legal barriers between social classes. The government built railroads, telegraph and postal systems, set up banks, and reformed the currency; permitted foreign travel, allowed newspapers and magazines to be published, and encouraged the idea that business was a respectable and desirable occupation. As a matter of fact, the emperor became a rich man by investing in business himself.

The chief opposition to Western customs and to the forced pace of industrialization came from the rural elements. But they were without power.

Japan needed capital to expand in all of these enterprises. Where could the capital come from, if not from foreign countries? But at this stage, in the 1880s–1890s the oligarchy refused to involve the country in heavy foreign loans on the grounds that this would also bring with it foreign control.

Meiji Land Tax

The money had to come from the only major source of revenue in an agricultural country—land taxes. Despite all efforts to establish industry since the Meiji Restoration, in the period between 1894–1904, agriculture was still Japan's economic base. Farming employed about 14 million people and concerned itself mainly with rice and raw silk. Rice production increased from thirty million koku (or bushels) in 1880, to forty-five million koku in 1904. The raw silk industry had grown even faster, from 11.5 million pounds in 1894 to 16.5 million pounds in 1904. There was also a proportionate increase in barley, wheat, and other crops. Although Japan was not able to compete with India in the production of cotton, her textile mills were in a period of rapid expansion. Japan, during this period, was necessarily a nation dependent on its agriculture. The tenant farmer, however, continued to pay his rent as a percentage of the main crop, a custom which worked to the advantage of the landlords and to the disadvantage of tenants. The tenant farmer was almost always in debt and therefore had to sell his rice crop long before harvest. And once in debt to a usurer, the peasant rarely got out again.

The depressed condition of the peasant class inevitably led to landlord–tenant disputes and sporadic peasant outbreaks.

The fact that the agricultural interests put up such a bitter struggle against the oligarchy in the first decade of the constitution was due mainly to the stresses and strains that came with the agricultural revolution.

While the battle was going on, it was inevitable that the growing commercialization of agriculture—the increase in size of holdings and consequent units of production, and gradual application of science and technology—would bring about an increase in rice production per unit of land cultivated.

The government took the initiative in making available to the farmer better seeds, implements, and the peasants supplied the needed capital through the land tax.

The political and economic problems were therefore inextricably intertwined—robbing the countryside in order to build up the towns.

About this time, the government offered to sell state properties to ex-Samurai groups, the discontented class at the time. The government hoped to divert and divide them. This plan to sell land met with opposition from the farm bloc in the first Diet.

The policies of the Meiji oligarchy tended to make the scale of land-holding considerable. As a result, the number of tenants increased and the number of landlords decreased. The hierarchy of ownership had many stages. There were those landlords who lived on the land and supervised their tenants; those who were landlords or even cultivators and half entrepreneurs in rural enterprises; absentee landlords; those who were part owners, part cultivators; those who were pure tenants, and, at the bottom of the scale, the landless peasants.

The simple device of demanding land tax in cash had

several consequences. Although the tax at first was actually lower than in Tokugawa times, it forced landlords to get cash and therefore to be catalysts in setting up rural banks, agricultural schools and experiment stations. Much government interest was motivated by the desire to secure goods for export; hence tea and silk production were encouraged and paid handsome dividends later on.

The government drive to mechanize industry was intensified during and after the Sino-Japanese War of 1894–1895. The government felt strong enough to accept foreign loans, which became necessary due to indebtedness and inflation caused by the war, and to assist the new industries so strongly desired by credits, subsidies, and protective legislation.

Rise of Industrial Power

The construction of heavy industry was stimulated to an even greater extent after the Sino-Japanese War by an increase in armament spending. The capital of the engineering industries rose from 2.6 million yen in 1893 to 14.6 million yen in 1903. Also by 1903, the shipping and shipbuilding industries had expanded so greatly that 35 percent of all the ships entering Japanese ports flew the Japanese flag. In 1896, the government decided to build iron and steel works to increase the production of domestic armaments so as to make Japan even more self-sufficient. By 1901, it was producing 243,000 tons of pig iron and 255,000 metric tons of steel. Also during this period, coal production rose from 5 million metric tons to 13 million. Electricity was readily available by 1900 for use in the expanding industries of Japan. From the information presented above, one can see that Japan was greatly expanding during the ten-year period of 1894 to 1904. The significance of this expansion is that by 1894, the Japanese had embarked on a policy of conquest, and instead of neglecting her industry, expanded even more. Probably the major cause or reason that Japan was able to keep expanding after the Sino-Japanese War was the indemnity of two hundred million taels she had received from China. This windfall had solved the financial crisis following the war.

Japanese capitalism developed, not as state capitalism nor as unfettered private enterprise, but as a unique combination of the two. The oligarchy had to find capital, select enterprises, train managers and workmen, secure the raw materials, and so forth. The government continued to direct, stimulate, subsidize, protect, and control—but not to own and manage—the industries except those important for purposes of warfare. Thus Japanese business came to depend on government policy and government aid and vice versa.

Two main reasons why business was peculiarly dependent on the government were:

1. The process of industrialization had to be forced on all by the power of the state; resources were limited and had to be expanded according to plan in order to avoid waste; the pressures of foreign powers were too great to be warded off by unprotected private enterprise.

2. The second reason was that the old commercial class which had grown up under Tokugawa rule did not reestablish economic leadership in spite of its important role in the Restoration. The leadership of the industrial movement came from the old warrior class. Why did the Samurai take the leadership?

The government leaders needed the Samurai, because they could be trusted to carry on the prestige of the warrior in spite of the fall of the Tokugawa. As a matter of fact, the ideology of the Meiji Restoration had been built up with such intuitive understanding. Selling government properties to Samurai at low prices was a good start.

The ruling oligarchy, who transferred to economics the view they had of politics, saw nothing unusual in the close association between political and economic forces. They did not want to restrict and control the power of government; rather they competed for its strong and paternalistic protection.

In spite of official encouraging of private enterprise, the structure of the Japanese economy was originally characterized by a high degree of centralization.

Zaibatsu enterprises were born during the time of the Restoration. The best known houses were Mitsui, Mitsubishi, Sumitomo, Yasuda. The zaibatsu played an important role in Japanese politics and economics. One may find a conflict of interest between Mitsui and Mitsubishi, but never between the government and the zaibatsu.

Zaibatsu Stronger than Before

The development of Japanese capitalism did not foster the emergence of a middle class. In addition to the zaibatsu, there were small businessmen, but their economic independence was limited by the fact that credit, management, and political influence were concentrated in the hands of the monopolistic zaibatsu. As the zaibatsu held the same theory of the state as the oligarchy, the lesser businessmen were not likely to challenge them.

Knowing the feudalistic economic system in prewar Japan, the Allied forces had attempted to democratize the economy during their early occupation of Japan. The monopolistic zaibatsu system, however, recovered as soon as the peace treaty was signed and gained new independence. The four zaibatsu—Mitsui, Mitsubishi, Sumitomo, and Yasuda—which dominated the Japanese economy by fixing prices, allocated markets, bought and sold Japanese governments, and dictated national policies. They were fattened by the war, and exercised restraints on international trade through various branches and connections all over the world. Zaibatsu were back in the saddle thanks to the American Occupation.

Each zaibatsu exercises central control through its banks and insurance companies. Each operates shipping lines, coal mines, armaments plants; runs factories, warehouses, and distribution facilities in almost all phases of industry and commerce; and of course, each has extensive overseas investments like all other cartels in the world. Each zaibatsu owns and controls about thirty basic industries encompassing all areas of the Japanese economy.

The system is clearly the antithesis of democracy. That is why General Douglas MacArthur, as commander of the Allied Occupation, ordered the zaibatsu dissolved in 1945, and forbade their participation in international cartels. The Japanese Diet subsequently enacted legislation putting his orders into effect. "The way has now been cleared for the first time in Japanese history for the Japanese people to achieve economic freedom," MacArthur declared. But before the occupation ended in 1952, the zaibatsu were allowed to reconsolidate, and the process was accelerated. A year after the Occupation forces had withdrawn, the Japanese Diet revised the antimonopoly laws, legalizing the reconstitution of the zaibatsu without any public notice or protest from the United States government. Something like forty separate laws have been enacted to encourage cartelism since that time.

There are six major zaibatsu groups today in Japan. They are Mitsui, Mitsubishi, Sumitomo, which have been restored—the Dai Ichi Bank group, Fuji Bank group, and Sanwa Bank group, which are products of the postwar period. Among three old zaibatsu groups, Mitsubishi became the leader due to its concentration in heavy chemicals; Mitsui is the second in rank, and Sumitomo follows closely behind it. The old Yasuda zaibatsu merged with the Fuji Bank group, while Dai Ichi Bank represents the old Kawajaki zaibatsu. Sanwa Bank represents a new zaibatsu in Japan.

It is important to examine subsidiary firms that either belong to or are controlled by the six zaibatsu groups.

A. Mitsubishi group. The total capital investment amounts to ¥2,739 or about $1 billion and total combined sales amount to $22 billion in 1973 alone. The major subsidiary firms are:[1] Mitsubishi Bank; Mitsubishi Trust Co.; Meiji Life Insurance Co.; Tokyo Marine Insurance Co.; Mitsubishi Mining Co.; Mitsubishi Copper Co.; Mitsubishi Metal Co.; Mitsubishi Electric Co.; Mitsubishi Chemical Co.; Mitsubishi Glass Co.; Mitsubishi Oil Co.; Mitsubishi Paper Co.; Mitsubishi Trading Co.; Mitsubishi Warehouse Co.; Mitsubishi Land Co.; Edokawa Chemical Co.; and any one of these companies is a leading firm in its respective field. For instance, Meiji Life Insurance Company is one of the largest insurance companies in Japan.

B. Mitsui group. The total combined capital which the Mitsui group invested in the following companies amounts to ¥1,351 (100 million unit) or about $5 billion, and the total amount of annual sales amounts to ¥8,356 (100 million unit) or about $3 billion.

The major subsidiary firms belonging to the Mitsui are:[2] Mitsui Bank; Mitsui Trust Co.; Mitsui Life Insurance Co.; Mitsui Mining Co.; Mitsui Metal Co.; Mitsui Shipbuilding Co.; Mitsui Chemical Co.; Mitsui Trading Co.; Mitsui Real Estate Co.; Mitsui Warehouse Co.; Mitsui Shipping Co.; Mitsui Construction Co.; Mitsui Agriculture-Forestry Co.; Osaka Shipping Co.; Showa Aircraft Co.; Japan Flour Mills; Tokyo

Cotton Co.; and ten others. All of these companies are leading firms in their respective fields.

C. Sumitomo group. The total capital of the combined firms amounts to ¥1,586 (100 million unit) or about $590 million and the total annual sales amount to ¥7,369 (100 million unit) or about $2.7 billion. Some of their major subsidiary firms are as follows:[3] Sumitomo Bank (world's 27th largest bank); Sumitomo Trust Co.; Sumitomo Life Insurance Co.; Sumitomo Marine Insurance Co.; Sumitomo Coal Co.; Sumitomo Mining Co.; Sumitomo Cement Co.; Sumitomo Metal Co.; Sumitomo Electric Co.; Sumitomo Chemical Co.; Sumitomo Machinery Co.; Sumitomo Trading Co.; Sumitomo Warehouse Co.; Sumitomo Real Estate Co.; and many others.

D. Dai-Ichi Bank group. The total capital investment amounts to ¥1,643 or about $600 million, and the total annual sales amount to ¥7,282 or about $2.6 billion. Some of the leading subsidiary firms are as follows:[4] Dai-Ichi Bank; Asahi Life Insurance Co.; Furukawa Mining Co.; Furukawa Electric Co.; Yokohawa Rubber Co.; Fuji Electric Co.; Nippon Light Metal Co.; Kawajaki Heavy Chemical Co.; Kawajaki Steel Co.; Kawajaki Electric Co.; Kawajaki Shipping Co.; Kawajaki Aircraft Co., and others.

E. The Fuji Bank group. The total capital investment amounts to ¥3,098 (100 million) or about $1.1 billion, and the total sales amount to ¥16,847 (100 million), about $6.2 billion. Some of the leading subsidiary firms are as follows:[5] Fuji Bank; Yasuda Trust Co.; Yasuda Life Insurance Co.; Yasuda Fire Insurance Co.; Oki Electric Co.; Kokusaku Pulp Co.; Showa Electric Co.; Showa Shipping Co.; Nissan Automobile Co.; Japan Airline Co.; Japan Refrigeration Co.; Japan Cement Co.; Hitachi Manufacturing Co.; Tokyo Construction Co.; Tokyo-Yokohama Railway Co.; and many others.

F. Sanwa Bank group. The total capital investment amounts to ¥3,454 (100 million unit) or about $1.2 billion, and the total annual sales amount to ¥16,501 (100 million) or about $6 billion. Some of the leading firms are as follows[6] Sanwa Bank; Toyo Trust Co.; Japan Life Insurance Co.; Nippon Rayon Co.; Nippon Textile Co.; Teijin Textile Co.; Kansai Paint Co.; Osaka Cement Co.; Nakayama Copper Co.; Hidachi Manufacturing Co.; Marujen Oil Co.; Hidachi Shipbuilding Co.; Toyo Rubber Co.; Nippon Transportation Co.; Takajimaya Department Store; and others.

There are few big companies not listed among the six groups. For instance, New Nippon Steel Company and Tokyo Electric are not controlled by one zaibatsu group, but by the combined group. Tokyo Electric is controlled by the combined forces of Mitsubishi and Mitsui, while Fuji Steel (now, New Nippon Steel) is controlled by both Fuji Bank and Mitsubishi zaibatsu.

Zaibatsu—Old and New

These six zaibatsu groups, either reconstructed or newly organized, differ from the old zaibatsu. The new groups are highly developed and well-organized compared with the old ones. The old zaibatsu concentrated their capital in industrial development, while the new groups are concentrated and controlled by finance capital rather than industrial capital. In other words, Japanese capitalism is comparable to the advanced capitalism of the West. Every one of these groups is headed by a bank. The bank controls them, rather than the companies controlling the bank. This has been even more true after 1955. City banks supplied the major share of funds, rather than the public financial institutions, for the expansion of the industries. Such funding was, of course, practiced with fierce competition among the city banks. In Table 8, one can see evidence of the competition.

Such furious competition was a characteristic of Japanese capitalism in the postwar era. It should be pointed out that over two-thirds of the amount on loan from the city banks was lent to large enterprises, as is clearly indicated by Table 9.

When we add up the amounts of loans made by the long-term credit banks, the trust banks, and the development banks, it becomes clear that an immense amount of capital funds is being supplied entirely for the purpose of financing large industries.

Another important point to look into in the zaibatsu situation is the area of small savings. The Japanese people have the habit of depositing money in the bank to accrue interest rather

Table 8

A Comparison of the Role of City Banks[7] and Securities Market in Financing Business

	Securities Market				Private Financial Institutions				
Year	Total external funds supplied	Shares	Debentures	Total	City banks	Long-term credit banks	Others	Government financial institutions	Finance special account
1954	100.0%	23.23	3.01	66.21	14.96	9.79	41.45	16.35	2.67
1955	100.0%	14.12	3.92	68.91	17.68	7.47	43.76	11.07	3.32
1956	100.0%	12.53	4.06	76.78	40.87	3.94	31.97	4.98	2.33
1957	100.0%	15.89	2.91	73.36	33.90	4.87	34.59	6.08	1.94
1958	100.0%	14.28	3.54	72.44	24.82	8.30	39.32	7.29	2.46
1959	100.0%	11.17	6.88	73.06	24.78	6.94	41.34	6.42	2.48
1960	100.0%	16.12	5.22	71.19	24.83	6.34	40.02	5.46	2.01

Table 9

Conditions of Business Loans in Japan[8]

Sources	Percentage
Private financial institutions:	
City banks	68.68
Local banks	36.61
Long-term loan and trust banks	86.39
Financial institutions for medium and smaller enterprises	10.31
Total Percentage	70.75%
Government financial institutions:	
Development bank	34.31%
Small business finance corporation	0.12
People's finance corporation	12.20
Total Percentage	37.64%
Business associates	16.39
Professional moneylenders	–
Relatives and acquaintances	0.78
Others, including foreign loans	59.44
Grand Total	58.04%

than investing in a speculative market. Such savings habits could probably be traced to the early days of the Meiji era when the government forced the people to save using a postal savings plan. The government used these long-term deposits for the development of new industries.

Most Japanese banks, controlled by the zaibatsu, take advantage of the savings tradition in accumulation of their capital. Financing the business through issuing stock and bonds is not popular in Japan. Consequently, the zaibatsu groups are making profits with ordinary citizens' savings, and do not return the proper share of profits to the investors.

In 1967, six major banks invested their capital in their subsidiaries in the following manner.[9]

Mitsui Bank invested 64.76 percent; Mitsubishi Bank, 52.23 percent; Sumitomo Bank, 59.53 percent; Fuji Bank, 43.48 percent; Dai Ichi Bank, 40.91 percent; and Sanwa Bank invested 46.64 percent.

In other words, the balance of the capital came from another source if their own banks were unable to finance their enterprise. Through the investment system, the banks control the companies, and the banks' capital is the accumulation of the people's savings.

Another characteristic of the new zaibatsu group is concentration in heavy chemical and electronics industries just as once they had concentrated in coal and iron industries. Such investment is supervised by the bank, directly or indirectly. The bankers dictate the companies' policies.

Role of Bank of Japan

On top of such concentrated loans by city banks to their zaibatsu groups, the Bank of Japan also played an important role in the formulation of the new zaibatsu groups in the postwar era. It was the Bank of Japan, as the central bank of the nation, which lent to the city banks. Actually, the city banks were very much dependent on the Bank of Japan. The industries built by old and new zaibatsu groups in postwar Japan could not possibly have developed on such a gigantic scale without the support of the Bank of Japan.

Table 10 indicates the comparative situation of central bank loans to private creditors among six nations.

Table 10

Principal Assets of Central Banks[10]
(end of 1962)

	United States	England	West Germany	France	Italy	Japan
Gold & Foreign Exchange	29.1%	0.01%	64.6%	34.2%	21.2%	13.8%
To Government credit	56.5	97.8	26.3	25.8	59.8	18.3
To Private credit	0.3	2.1	8.0	36.0	17.7	62.2
Others	14.1	0.0	1.1	4.0	1.3	5.7
	100%	100%	100%	100%	100%	100%

According to Table 10, Japan provides 62.2 percent of the private credit. This is due to increased loans to the city banks by the Bank of Japan, which is government-owned. The advantage of such huge loans to city banks by the central bank is the extremely low interest rate, and large enterprises that do not associate with the zaibatsu arenot able to benefit from the Bank of Japan. Consequently, zaibatsu-owned enterprises are in a better position to invest in new businesses since the city banks can borrow immense sums at low interest rates from the central bank. In other words, the government-owned central bank promoted big business more than ever before by the allocation of huge loans for city banks with low rates of interest.

Six major city banks, closely associated with the old and new zaibatsu groups, borrowed about $750 million in September 1960. The Mitsui Bank, one of the six, borrowed some $147 million, which was about 11 percent of that bank's funds supplied by the Bank of Japan. This amount increased to about $370 million or about 22 percent for the Mitsui Bank in September, 1961.

All city banks in Japan borrowed about $3.5 billion from the Bank of Japan in September 1961, while the six major city banks—Mitsui, Mitsubishi, Sumitomo, Fuji, Sanwa, Dai-Ichi—borrowed about $2.1 billion.[11] In other words, the amount, $2.1 billion, the six zaibatsu banks borrowed from the Bank of Japan was more than half of the total amount, $3.5 billion.

A Japanese economist summed up the situation in the

following statement:

> In this way this principle of equality, linked with the pipe lines of the powerful banks, has become "built-in" as one of the principal institutional factors in investment behavior aiming set control by the Keiretsu.[12]

Such a system is closely related with the new concept of "liberalization." Liberalization was inevitable due to American participation in the Japanese economy. According to Japanese official reports, about 61 percent of the foreign firms in Japan belong to the United States, and eighty-three out of 200 major American corporations are engaged in business in Japan today. For instance, twelve out of twenty-three major American electric firms; eleven out of twenty major American petroleum companies; ten out of sixteen major American chemical companies; and, six out of seven major American pharmaceutical manufacturers are operating in Japan as of 1970. The petroleum industry is especially significant in view of its size and control. It controls more than a half of the Japanese market. Standard Oil is, not surprisingly, the leader.[13]

More recently, the major impact on the Japanese economy has been the automobile industry. Since a significant portion of American consumers prefer to buy smaller cars like the Volkswagen and others, and because American car-makers have been unable to attract them with domestic models, the automotive complex's response has been to buy into the foreign car industry, especially in Japan. For instance, Chrysler went with the Mitsubishi-Zaibatsu group; General Motors with Isuzu; while Ford tied in with Toyo Kogyo. The two largest companies, Toyota and Nissan, held more than 70 percent of the domestic Japanese market and 90 percent of the export market.[14] The American automotive industry intends to challenge these markets in the future. Why should the Japanese government allow such foreign competition that is adverse to the Japanese firms? There is no choice for Japan at the present time, since she is still a junior partner to American capitalism in Asia. This situation becomes more apparent in the political arena than in the economic field.

Managerial Elite

Unlike the old zaibatsu system, the new zaibatsu groups are now under the domination of finance capital. A few members among the ruling class succeeded in dominating the bank and industry, in combination. Such powerful economic groups also control the political power of the nation. Three major zaibatsu groups controlled the political power of Japan before her defeat in World War II, but the political structure has changed somewhat in postwar Japan.

First of all, the powerful figures who ran three major zaibatsu groups have stayed behind the actual manipulation of the system since managerial power has emerged. The professional bankers, rather than the key figures of the old zaibatsu groups, now run the show. This situation was created by the combined efforts of the key figures of the old zaibatsu groups and the government high officials. There is no conflict of interest. They were responsible for the reconstruction of the postwar Japanese economy with the aid of the United States. American capital played an essential role in this process. Nippon Kogyo, the Japanese Industrial Club, includes members who are the top managerial officers of the important banks and presidents of big companies, and has become the most important institution of the Japanese economy. The major economic decisions of postwar Japan were decided at this club. Another important economic organization is, of course, the Association of Economic Organizations or Keijai Tantai Rengokai. The advisory council of this association consists of the key decision-makers in the financial world.

The Japanese government and politics are subordinate to these economic organizations. The political organization has made use of the same tactics and practices as the Meiji Restoration. For instance, not only do government funds support these economic organizations, but members select their own representatives for important government offices, including the cabinet, the policy committee of the Bank of Japan, the Central Bank, and others.

As powerful as they are, these six major zaibatsu groups are still subordinate to American capitalism. Without American support and cooperation, their economic development and growth would be faced with an immediate crisis. Raw materials and markets, both in the United States and Southeast Asia, are available to Japan only when the American capitalists are willing to share them. How long Japanese capitalism will follow such a course is a matter of great concern to Americans as well as to the Japanese.

Economic Dependence Feared

How long will Mitsubishi Heavy Industries rely on Douglas, North American, and Lockheed? How long will Kawasaki Aircraft take orders from Boeing and Bell? How long will Fuji Heavy Industries rely on Beech, Cessna, and Bell? How long will Ishikawajima-Harima rely on General Electric? How long will Teijin Seiki, which makes jet engine parts and flight control systems, be satisfied with Bendix, Lear, and Ziegler? Will Litton Industries control Tokyo Shibaura Electric indefinitely? In 1970, Japan's balance of payments amounted to some $400 million, and this figure had doubled since 1967. A very large proportion, probably 70 percent, must have gone to the United States according to the technical agreements signed with foreign interests.

The amount of the foreign investment has varied from year to year. In the years of 1952, 1959 and 1960, the amount declined. In 1957, foreign investment amounted to over $100 million, but the amount increased to almost $400 million in 1961.

What is important is not the amount but how much American capital controls Japanese finances. The amount of American capital investment in Japan was equal to ten times that of the Japanese in the United States as of 1971. But even this situation does not reveal the true picture of Japanese subordination to American corporations.

What sort of industries did foreign capital invest in? Table 11 indicates the kinds of investment Americans and other foreign companies made in Japan from 1949 to 1967.

It becomes evident that American surplus capital looked for overseas investment for various reasons, and found in Japan a most favorable situation. Another clear picture emerges—new capital, mostly American, was invested primarily in new industries—including electronics, heavy chemical, petroleum,

Table 11

Foreign Capital Investment in Japan[15]
(1949 to 1967)

Type of Industry	Technical Investment	Stock Investment with Managerial Participation		Direct Loan	
	Projects	Projects	Amount	Projects	Amount*
Electronic Machine Manufacturing	926	....	....	....	....
Transportation Machine Manufacturing	168	349	8,136	272	55,801
Other Machine Manufacturing	1,581	....	....	....	....
Metal Industry	378	52	2,345	147	58,982
Chemical Industry	981	176	8,686	183	36,594
Textile Industry	184	34	239	64	10,146
Oil Industry	103	46	9,478	83	56,675
Rubber, Leather Manufacturing	76	25	1,528	....	....
Glass Manufacturing	93	22	677	....	....
Construction	66	8	46	24	48,331
Paper Industry	52	....	....	7	610
Mining Industry	....	....	....	12	21,247
Transportation	....	20	61	114	58,217
Electricity/Gas	....	....	....	61	65,850
Warehouse	....	1	0.6	7	212
Trade	....	175	1,335	19	853
Service Industry	....	33	83	....	....
Food Industry		20	675		
Insurance	....	....	....	18	2,785
Others	165	50	1,160	88	9,975
Total	4,773	1,011	34,407	1,099	410,156

*10,000 unit

transportation, electricity. These identify closely with that of a war economy.

It was, therefore, not an accident that Japan became a chief supplier for the Vietnam war on behalf of the United States.

For example, at the time of American escalation in Vietnam in 1965, Japan exported to Vietnam and vicinity about $95.6 million worth of goods. A year later, as the war escalated more rapidly, Japanese exports also increased rapidly. The amount was increased more than ten times in 1966, and more than thirteen times in 1967. The Japanese economy prospered because of the Vietnam war just as it did during the Korean war in 1950. War and a capitalistic economy have an inseparable relationship in both the United States and Japan.

Table 12 on Japanese exports during the Vietnam war supports such a thesis.

Table 12

Japanese Exports and Vietnam War[16]
(figures in $ million)

	1965	1966	1967
Direct Export Goods	$16.0	$147.0	$ 206.0
Indirect Export Goods	79.6	836.7	1,169.3
Export to U.S.A.	....	456.5	522.3
Export to Vietnam Vicinity	79.6	875.2	647.0
Total	$95.6 million	$978.7 million	$1.4 billion

Can the Japanese economy prosper without the Vietnam war? Can any capitalistic economy prosper without war? Will the Japanese business community remain under the subjugation of the Americans? When the struggle between Japanese and American capitalism becomes desperate, what then?

Militarism will be restored in order to protect Japanese business interests in South Korea, and Southeast Asia. Will such Japanese militarism become a threat to peace in Asia again?

Are the leaders of the People's Republic of China and the Democratic People's Republic of Korea overly sensitive about the restoration of Japanese militarism?

The American policy has been to rebuild Japan as a military power, as its watchdog in Asia. Is this policy going to support American interests in the long run? In order to find some answers to these many questions, we will attempt to analyze Japanese economic activities in the 1970s and the present situation in the next chapter.

Notes

1. Compiled from *Nenpo* or *Year Book,* "The Study of Holding Company," *Hompō Keizai Tōkei or Hompō Economic Statistics,* and *Asia Trend Year Book,* 1970, Tokyo. Present exchange ratio of yen is about ¥268–270 to $1.

2. Ibid.

3. Ibid.

4. Ibid.

5. Ibid.

6. Ibid.

7. Compiled from Statistics Department, the Bank of Japan, *Hompō Keizai Tōkei* or *Economic Statistics of Japan,* 1962. Quoted in Yoshikazu Miyazaki's "Rapid Economic Growth in Postwar Japan" in *Comparative National Economic Policies* by William Moskoff (Boston: D.C. Heath, 1973), p. 122.

8. Ibid., p. 124.

9. *Nenpo* or *Year Book,* "The Study of Holding Company," p. 13.

10. Miyazaki, "Rapid Economic Growth," P. 134.

11. Figures are based on *Hompō Keizai Tōkei.*

12. Miyazaki, p. 136.

13. John G. Roberts, "The American Zaibatsu" of *FEER* 5, January 30, 1971.

14. Jon Holliday and Gavan McCormack, *Japanese Imperialism Today* (London: Assn. for Radical East Asian Studies), p. 3.

15. Keizai Chosa Kyokai, *Foreign Investment Overview According to the Industries,* Tokyo, 1969.

16. Nomura Research Institute, *The End of Vietnam War and Japanese Export Business* Tokyo, 1969.

9 American Aid to Japanese Imperialism

J. A. Hobson, a British economist, explained in his renowned book, *Imperialism,* that British imperialism was more or less synonymous with colonialism or mercantilism. Britain acquired colonies as sources of raw material, as a dumping ground for surplus capital, and as a market for manufactured goods. Unable to find profitable enterprises at home, British capitalists sought and found them abroad. British overseas investments rose from 785 million pounds in 1871 to 3.5 billion pounds in 1911. Lenin supported Hobson's view and said that "under modern capitalism, when monopolies prevail, the export of capital has become a typical feature."[1]

The United States gave direct aid of some $2 billion in the first year of the Occupation and indirect aid through the plan of procurement expenditures during the Korean war of twice that amount. But when it comes to investments, American contributions in Japan amounted to only $676 million in 1965. The figure is, comparatively speaking, low and also deceptive. Where the American capitalists made their investments and how they are influencing Japan's basic industries are the significant issues.

Japanese capitalists have found themselves in what they call a "river of no return." They cannot go back to the river they have already crossed if they wish to remain in the international race of capitalistic competition. In order to identify herself as a competitor, Japan has also perpetrated the liberalization of investment. Foreign capitalists, primarily Americans, are free to invest in Japan, and the Japanese capitalists are free to invest abroad, including the United States. The Japanese began their investment program in Alaska and elsewhere in the United States in the last few years.

Economic Expansion Liberalized

To compete with American business in American-dominated markets is a new and different kind of competition for Japanese businessmen. As long as Japan and the United States agreed to divide the market and sphere of economic influence, and each side observed the rules and regulations, there would be temporary stability and peace. Monopolistic capitalism, however, cannot be controlled with restraints too long, as we have witnessed periodically in recent history.

The reason why Japan became a prosperous economic state with the help of American aid is quite obvious. "The export of capital greatly affects and accelerates the development of capitalism in those countries to which it is exported. While, therefore, the export of capital may tend to a certain extent to arrest development in the countries exporting capital, it can only do so by expanding and deepening the further development of capitalism throughout the world."[2]

This is what is happening now in Japan. Both in Japan and the United States, this inflationary policy has been employed, consequently having a negative effect on technological advancement, and has brought economic stagnation from time to time. In order to overcome such a slowdown, Japanese capitalists, as well as their American partners, needed to liberalize their investment policy and trade policy on a worldwide scale.

The tremendous development of postwar Japanese economic power was due to the Japanese capitalists who undertook three major areas of concentration. First of all, they regained their former markets in Asia and much needed new ones with the help of the American government since the Occupation in

1945. Secondly, Japanese capitalists intensified their merger plan, especially in the 1960s. Thirdly, the Japanese government has been restoring Japanese militarism in order to protect their economic interests in the future.

Not only has it been the official policy of Japan to support the monopoly system in the postwar era, but many well-known Japanese economists, for example, Professor Ishizaka, have advocated the end of Japan's monopoly law, which is similar to the Sherman Antitrust Act. He said that "there is no company big enough to be considered as a monopoly in Japan. . . ."[3] The implication here is that the big monopolies do not threaten the Japanese economy, and furthermore it is advantageous to have such companies in order to compete with foreign giants.

Mergers and Monopoly

In spite of a threat to the national economy, the increasing numbers of mergers since 1960 have been a major trend in the Japanese economy. There were about 300–400 mergers until 1960, but the number increased to 500 in 1961; 715 in 1962; 997 in 1963; 864 in 1964; 894 in 1965, and more than 1000 both in 1967 and 1968. The amount of capital involved in these mergers in forty-four instances was about Y100 million each, and nine mergers dealt with over Y1,000 million in 1964 alone.

The mergers were most active among the manufacturing, retailing, and service industries from 1964, and more than 44 percent of the total of 1020 mergers were classified as manufacturing industry in 1968. Retailing and wholesale businesses accounted for 22 percent, while transportation and communication were in third place with 11.5 percent. Among the manufacturing industries, the machinery business was the leader, and the food, chemical, oil, coal, and textile industries followed.

Why did the mergers become so active and popular within Japanese industry? Why did the government so actively support such a policy? The simple answer is that Japanese industry at all levels needed to compete with foreign challenges effectively in order to advance. That was an official position of the government. The public policy and big business policy were identical. For instance, the two biggest steel companies of Japan, Yahata Steel and Fuji Steel, merged in 1970 with official government blessing. They merged to combine their strength and so as to compete with the American steel producers. The Japanese government promoted such activity by allowing all sorts of advantages for the mergers. In 1965, when the Prince Automobile Company was suffering from poor profits, reaching a low of 1.6 percent dividend, the Department of Trade initiated a negotiation to merge Prince and Nissan through the companies' banks—Nippon Kogyo and Sumitomo.

Interestingly enough, when certain business groups registered complaints about the steel giants' merger, Chairman Yamata of the Federal Fair Practices Commission, whose job it was to prevent monopoly (according to the old monopoly law, Article 15), commented that there are bad monopolies, and good monopolies. Not all monopoly, therefore, should be regulated by law. He believed that the merger of Yahata and Fuji was a good one, and would not endanger the steel industry in spite of the fact that their combined output would be more than a half of the total steel production in Japan. An editorial in *Yomiuri* on February 25, 1969, one of the leading Japanese daily newspapers, in reference to Chairman Yamata's comment, said:

> . . . public officials seem to minimize about the restoration of competition as much as possible. They don't attempt to interpret the Monopoly Law with consistency, and do not judge the merger of large enterprises from such perspective. Aren't these mergers approved by the public office under political pressures? We feel that the public office has lost its reason to exist by the judgment they gave out this time.[4]

In spite of protests from the workers, students, and the press, the merger of the two steel giants continued with the support of the government, the Liberal-Democratic Party, which controls the present government, and, of course, the financial circle. The New Japan Steel Corporation was thus born on March 31, 1970. The historical competition between the two rivals ended there, and the new company moved into the field of international competition, especially in the American market.

Japan's Powerful Steel Industry

Japanese business had a special interest in the development of the steel industry in the postwar era. Starting from 1951, the capital investment in steel amounted to Y753 billion, or about $21.5 billion, during the subsequent ten years. This astronomical investment has continued to the present time. For instance, Japan invested Y800 billion in capital improvement in 1969 but Y491 billion in 1968. Yahata and Fuji, of course, led such gigantic capital improvements.[5]

As a result, steel production in Japan became a sort of American success story in the postwar period. Yahata Steel occupied the position of the fifth largest steel producer in the world in 1968. With the merger of Fuji Steel in 1970, total sales volume was more than $2.7 billion compared to U. S. Steel's $4.5 billion, and Bethlehem Steel with $2.8 billion. With her ultramodern facilities, it would be easy for the New Japan Steel Company to outproduce second-ranking Bethlehem Steel in the near future.

There are, of course, other giants like Mitsubishi Heavy Industry Company, Nissan, Hitachi, Toyota, and others who are eager to export their steel products to the world market.

How was such a miracle possible in the Japanese economy, especially in heavy industries such as steel, automobiles, aircraft, and chemicals? Such a miracle was possible only because American policy made it possible. It started with the Dodge Plan in 1949. The Dodge Plan stressed several points in order to promote economic recovery in postwar Japan—some suggestions were a reduction in the number of factory workers, decreased wages, as well as an increase in factory output. Another important factor was the Korean war in 1950, an event that turned the Japanese economy into a war economy.

The Japanese government was also perfectly willing to cooperate with the business groups in the strengthening of these industries. For instance, there was a reduction of tax on capital accumulation; no tax on important machinery needed to build new factories; special privileges in the export industry; encouragement of mergers; and above all, protection of the privileged class, the elite companies of the zaibatsu group.

The zaibatsu, especially the three giants—Mitsubishi,

Mitsui, Sumitomo—are intensifying their merger activity. They are out to dominate Japan once again. For example, Mitsubishi enjoyed $22 billion in sales in 1973. This figure is about half the size of the national budget of Japan. Through its network of some 250 companies, 120 of them outside Japan, Mitsubishi has doubled its income since 1969. In 1973, its rate of growth rose by 33 percent or three times the rate of Japan's gross national product. Profits soared to $88 million.

Mitsubishi handled 13 percent of all national imports and 9 percent of exports in 1973. The top six companies handle about 50 percent of Japanese imports and 40 percent of its exports, and 20 percent of total domestic wholesale business. Not even the government can control these companies' influence in business.

Mitsubishi handles about 20,000 different lines of goods through its organizations beginning with manufacturing, then retailing. With more than 250 companies, one can imagine the variety of business with which it is involved. Does this bigness benefit the national economy of Japan? During the oil crisis at the end of 1973, wholesale prices jumped 35 percent and consumer prices went up 23 percent. It was considered the worst economic situation of all the industrialized nations. An American liberal and one time New Dealer, David Lilienthal, defended big business of America in 1953 by saying that " . . . from my own experiences, I conclude that Big Businesses are indispensable to our society. Accordingly, I believe that our national laws, our national climate of opinion, and the attitude of our public servants should be consistent with that conclusion."[6] Based on his experiences in public service, especially as the administrator of TVA and as chairman of the Atomic Energy Commission, Mr. Lilienthal defended big business in the United States as a desirable and a good thing. He pointed to a responsible businessman like the late Leroy Wilson, then president of American Telephone and Telegraph, and found that big business is also eager to commit itself to important defense work. Because of this eagerness, and their capabilities, Mr. Lilienthal believed that big business was indeed favorable to American national interests. There is something similar about David Lilienthal and Chairman Yamata of Japan. They are both good servants of the big business system.

Capitalistic Systems Differ

There are, of course, some differences between the American and Japanese systems. Big business in Japan is more open about its dealings with the Japanese government while business interests in the United States are rather secretive about sharing their plans with the American government and political groups. The political scandals between the Republican Party, the milk fund, and political contributions of International Telephone and Telegraph and many other large corporations are cases in point. This difference is due to the nature of the society involved.

How close are finance capital and industrial organizations among the zaibatsu groups in Japan? We mentioned earlier that the postwar Japanese industries were rigidly dominated by the banks. This is also a characteristic of the modern Japanese economy.

At the end of 1968, the Mitsubishi Bank financed 57 percent of its investments and financing to 145 companies which belonged to the Mitsubishi group. A similar concentration was found with the other zaibatsu groups—the Mitsui Bank financed 63.89 percent of the entire financing to 115 companies which belonged to the Mitsui group, and the Sumitomo Bank financed 52.58 percent of the financing to 98 companies which belong to the Sumitomo group.[7] Thus, three major zaibatsu groups were completely dominated by three major banks. We should also emphasize that most of the capital funds are derived from the public through their savings in banks. Approximately 40 percent of capital funds are secured with such savings, and only 4 percent of all capital funds are raised by selling stock, and less than 2 percent is involved with foreign capital. The rest was managed within the zaibatsu system itself.[8]

The second characteristic of the monopolistic zaibatsu group is that their mergers have been encouraged by the Japanese government, not only those between zaibatsu groups themselves, but among outsiders, including their present competitors in the market. Consequently, the elimination of competition among companies, and the building of monopolies in order to invade foreign markets, have been encouraged. The implication is significant and the merger of Yahata and Fuji is a good example. The role of the government does not limit this, but promotes individual savings in the banks, and these savings are, of course, used as long–term capital investment. This policy is successful because the stock market does not attract the Japanese as it does the Americans. The Japanese people would rather save their money than buy stocks. This is probably why the government had to step in in order to serve the zaibatsu groups. Pursuing such a policy results in two things: one is to strengthen the position of the zaibatsu, and the second is to exploit the masses without their knowing it.

Japan's soaring economy ranked third in the world in 1974, exceeded in size only by the United States and by the U.S.S.R. A vigorous industrialization drive enabled Japan to reach eighth place in 1950 and sixth a decade ago, overtaking the advanced economies of Western Europe, also approaching, and, in some sectors, surpassing, the U.S. and the U.S.S.R. Many observers project a continuation of the GNP of at least 10 percent annually to a total of some $500 billion by 1980. Predictions such as this might well be realized, but such forecasts might well turn out to be somewhat optimistic. At any rate, what we are concerned with is not the growth of Japan's economy in the 1980s, but the exploitation of the people for the sake of that growth.

Table 13 gives a picture of Japanese working-class mobility since 1950.

Table 13 indicates that the social structure of the Japanese population has changed significantly in the postwar era. The increasing numbers of industrial workers are unmistakable. The increase was sharper in 1960, when the United States and Japan signed a Mutual Security Treaty, and the monopolists moved into the Japanese business world with more aggression. As the defeated nation in the war, even the Japanese leaders were cautious about their business activities until they were assured of the support of their own as well as the American government. The growing numbers of the working class, about 30 million in 1970, however, pose a serious challenge to the ruling class of Japan. The increase is attributed mainly to youth and women. The youth group, in their twenties, is concentrated primarily in heavy chemical industries, while the women workers are in lighter industries. When asked why they seek

Table 13

The Change of Japanese Workers in Postwar Era[9]
(units in millions)

Class	1950	%	1955	%	1960	%	1965	%
Capitalist and Semicapitalist	102	2.8	124	3.1	167	3.8	233	4.8
Workers in cities	521	14.4	620	15.5	661	15.1	740	15.3
Farmers and Fishermen	1619	44.6	1505	37.7	1349	30.6	1110	23.0
Working Class	1389	38.2	1742	43.7	2224	50.5	2746	56.9
Labor population	3631	100	3991	100	4401	100	4829	100

Workers in cities—refers to workers who live in cities like Tokyo that are independent of political structures like Washington, D.C., but unlike New York City, which is part of New York State.

Working class—refers to workers employed in industries.

Labor population—refers to the combined population of all those engaged in production, including management.

jobs, Japanese housewives say that their husbands' wages are not adequate to support the family.

Rise of Labor Unions

The most powerful organized labor group, known as Sohyo or the General Council of Japanese Labor Unions, claimed a membership of nearly four million. Sohyo supports the Socialist party, and it has been more political than any other labor group. It has taken a strong and aggressive stand in favor of neutrality and advocates that Japan revoke her Mutual Security Treaty with the United States; that American military bases in Japan be removed as well as nuclear weapons, and that the power of the military forces be reduced.

Another labor group, known as Domei or the General Council of Japan Labor Organizations (formerly called Zenro), represents a membership of about a million and a half. It is considered middle-of-the-road in politics and concentrates on economic matters. This group supports the Democratic Socialist party. Other individual unions and associations actively engaged in politics are Nikkyoso or the Japanese Teachers' Union, and Zengakuren or the National Association of Student Self-Government Associations. As a whole, the total membership of organized labor amounted to more than 11 million in 1974. The ruling class of Japan can no longer ignore labor's growing power. For example, the trade unions gained an increase of 20–25 percent in annual wages in their 1974 spring collective bargaining throughout the country. When these groups get together and become politically active, they will exert a powerful influence on Japan's future. Knowing that such a threat exists, and in order to avoid such confrontation, the ruling class of Japan has begun again to build a large police and military force adequate to control domestic disturbances and eventually to protect their markets abroad just as they had done before.

Actual rearmament began in Japan when the Korean war broke out in June 1950. General MacArthur authorized the formation of a Keisatsu Yobitai, or a National Police Reserve, of 75,000 with a budget of 31 billion yen. General MacArthur allowed some thousands of former Japanese imperial troops, well-trained and eager to serve, to join the National Police system.

In 1952, the allocation was increased to 59 billion yen. Also in 1952, there was an additional appropriation of 65 billion yen for national defense payments, which included what was known as Japan's defense-share contribution. This was the expense borne by Japan for supplying equipment and services to American troops stationed in Japan under the Administrative Agreement signed by Japan and the United States on February 28, 1952. In 1954, Japan had to pay $155 million in accordance with the Mutual Defense Assistance Agreement which replaced the Administrative Agreement of 1952.

"Self-Defense" Forces

In the meantime, the National Police Reserve had been changed into the National Safety Force on October 15, 1952, under the jurisdiction of the National Safety Board established on August 1, while the responsibility for defending Japan against direct outside aggression remained with the American forces. In February 1953, the Keidanren or the Federation of Economic Organizations, a zaibatsu organization, announced a plan of rearmament in Tokyo. The plan was to build an army of 300,000 men; a navy of 290,000 tons and 70,000 men; an air force of 3750 planes and 130,000 men.

Then in September 1953, Prime Minister Yoshida gained support of the Progressives, the second largest political party in Japan at that time, in the belief that the new Japanese Constitution did not bar a proposed defense force. Thus on July 1, 1954, two laws further entrenched the self-defense forces and created what was, in effect, a ministry of defense. The first law was the Defense Agency Establishment Law. It set up the present defense organ under the office of the prime minister. A second statute, the Self-Defense Forces Law, reorganized the land and sea components and added a new air force.

Masuhara Keikichi, the first director-general of the National Police Reserve headquarters and vice-director-general of the new defense agency, summed up the purpose of the Defense Agency in these words:

> The purpose of the Defense Agency is to protect the peace and independence of our country and to safeguard its security. For this purpose it has as its mission to supervise, manage, and handle all matters concerning the Ground Self-Defense Force, the Maritime Self-Defense Force and the Air-Self-Defense Force.[10]

In 1955, the Japanese government agreed to increase her defense budget every year for three years to build a defense establishment. The Defense Council, legally organized in 1956, is composed of the prime minister, the finance minister, the defense board director-general, and the economic planning board director. The purpose of the agency is to advise the prime minister on basic principles of national defense.

Thus in 1956, the National Defense Council had been established and there were more than 180,000 men in uniform, trained by American military advisers in Japan and the United States. American military assistance was extended in the amount of $700 million and the Defense Force, though small in numbers, was declared to be "combat ready, capable of using the latest equipment and facilities."

In 1957, under Prime Minister Kishi, the Japanese-American Committee on Security was set up. Kishi openly discussed the possibility of Japan's acquiring nuclear weapons for the first time. Kishi proclaimed: "Not all nuclear weapons can be considered as falling within the purview of this prohibition [reference to Article 9 of the new Japanese Constitution]. If there is a nuclear weapon that can be considered as solely a defensive weapon, then it is not outside the realm of possibility for Japan to possess it."[11] Kishi was a prominent war criminal, but he had been cleansed, although he was not popular with the younger generation. The postwar generation believed in a democratic Japan, and wanted to maintain a peaceful and neutral Japan as declared in Article 9 of the Constitution. They were dead set against Kishi's idea of nuclear weapons for Japan. Prime Minister Kishi promoted, nevertheless, the Japanese defense program with the help of the United States. During his visit to Washington in June 1957, Kishi insisted that Japan should participate as a partner in the mutual defense of Japan and that Japan should have a voice in the use of American military forces stationed in Japan. Prime Minister Kishi became an outstanding anticommunist leader, the best kind of credentials to present to the American government. He advocated a policy of a partnership with the United States as the basis for a realistic national security policy for Japan. Japan was in no position to reject the protection of the United States, he believed. The issue of Japan's partnership with the United States became a crucial one in 1960. The Socialist party led an all-out campaign to oppose Kishi's position. Over 13 million Japanese signed a petition urging the dissolution of the Diet that supported Kishi's position, and called for a new election. The situation in Tokyo was so tense that Kishi had to cancel President Eisenhower's visit to Japan in June 1960, and then announced his own resignation. The new security treaty between the two nations came into effect on June 23, in spite of much violent objection among the Japanese.

Interestingly enough, the chief of staff of the new Japanese armed forces was General Genda Minoru, the main architect of the Pearl Harbor attack in 1941 and a key adviser to Admiral Yamamoto, who led the war against the United States in the Pacific.

In December 1965, the issue of nuclear weapons was

discussed again in the Japanese Diet. A high-level government spokesman stated that nuclear arms were permissible under the new Japanese Constitution if the weapons were for defense purposes only. Prime Minister Sato, like his predecessor Kishi, endorsed the statement officially.

Nuclear Power?

In May 1972, Kenichi Kitamura, commander of the Japanese Self-Defense Navy, declared at a news conference in Tokyo that Japan should have nuclear-powered submarines and attack aircraft carriers for "conducting operations in the oceans." This was an open declaration of a plan to rearm the Japanese navy with nuclear weapons.

Japanese militarists are encouraging arming the Self-Defense Forces with weapons of mass destruction and long-range attacking weapons and largely beefing up the naval force, in particular, along with the air force under the fourth "five-year Defense Build-up Plan."

What does the new Constitution say about this?

The preamble reads: "We, the Japanese people, desire peace for all time and are deeply conscious of the high ideals controlling human relationships, and we have determined to preserve our security and existence trusting in the justice of the peace loving people of the world." Then, in the famous Article 9, it also states that "land, sea, and air forces, as well as other war potentials, will never be maintained. The right of belligerency of the state will not be recognized."

How political leaders like Sato and Kishi can advocate the possession of nuclear weapons, an act that clearly contradicts the letter and spirit of the Constitution, cannot be comprehended, unless one understands the complete corruption of their political and moral activities. A policy of pacifism, the keystone of the original policy of occupied Japan, is not even mentioned by the ruling class of Japan today.

With the advance of technology, Japanese research on nuclear energy has been extensive, and she was the fourth nation to launch a space satellite, after only the U.S., the U.S.S.R., and France. In the field of weapons, Japan has the latest types: sixty-one tanks, heavy artillery, transport helicopters, F-104 supersonic jet fighters, Nike Hercules antiaircraft missiles, and destroyer escorts especially equipped for antisubmarine warfare.[13]

Besides those advanced weapons, Japan was making 97 percent of its own ammunition, 84 percent of its aircraft, tanks, guns, naval craft, and other military equipment by the end of 1969.[14]

The size of the Japanese armed forces is deceptive because of the heavy concentration of officers. These could be expanded on short notice by four to five times. For instance, there were about 250,000 men in the armed forces as of 1962. Four times that number is one million. With all the veterans of the Pacific and Asian wars, the Japanese armed forces could be one of the largest and most powerful at the present time. Japanese superiority in naval and air force strength is only superseded by the U.S. and the U.S.S.R.

The purpose of the military build-up in Japan is, first of all, to control domestic disorders and insurrections that have come about by increased awareness on the part of the working class of their exploitation. The second purpose of the military revival is to influence, intimidate, and control Japanese neighbors such as Korea, the Philippine Islands, other Southeastern Asian nations, even China.

In a recent election in July, 1974, the governing Liberal-Democrats, a conservative party, received another setback. This trend has continued over a decade in which the conservatives have continuously lost popularity. The political trend cast doubt on how much longer the Liberal Democrats can continue their quarter-century of political dominance.

In the upper house, since the July election, there are now sixty-two seats occupied by the Socialist party. The Komeito party, another mass-based party, has twenty-four seats, the Communist party has twenty seats, and the Democratic Socialists hold ten seats. In reality, the Liberal-Democratic party has only a slim majority of six seats or 129 out of 252 members. Compared with the last upper house election in 1971, the governing party lost 4.4 percent of total votes even after Prime Minister Tanaka had received much campaign support from the zaibatsu groups with their vast financial resources. The working class and the intellectuals once again supported opposition parties at this election. This is indeed a threat to the establishment.

Japan Eyes Korea Again

Korea is, of course, the first target of Japanese militarism just as it was at the end of the nineteenth century. The Nixon-Sato communiqué of November 1969 is a naked exposition of imperialistic dreams. Prime Minister Sato claimed publicly that Japan was willing to send her troops into South Korea if it was necessary to defend Japanese national interests. How can one be more frank than that? It is already a recognized fact that the United States has recognized South Korea as a "Japanese advance stronghold," as Nakasone, Japanese director-general of the Self-Defense Forces, has referred to Korea. Isn't this a repeat of the Taft-Katsura Agreement?[15] General Il-kwon Chung, the former premier of South Korea, said on the occasion of the Japan-Korea Treaty that if there was another war in Korea, he believed Japanese troops would be there to help the South Korean troops.[16]

In 1969, when the former prime minister of Japan visited President Park Chung-hee of South Korea in Seoul, Park asked Mr. Kishi a question concerning the Vietnam war. The visitor commented that the United States would eventually withdraw from Southeast Asia, and South Korea, too. To such an observation made by Kishi, President Park said, "Japan is the only nation that can be trusted in Asia."[17]

The situation in Asia has changed drastically since the end of World War II in 1945. The revival of Japanese militarism is a reality in Asia today. In view of this changed situation, both Premier Kim Il-sung of North Korea and Premier Chou En-lai of China were alarmed and issued a joint communiqué in Pyongyang on the twenty-first anniversary of the Korean Democratic People's Republic on September 8, 1969, to the effect that Japanese militarism was once again threatening peace in Asia.

The revival of Japanese militarism will not only threaten peace in Asia, but will equally threaten peace and order in American life. The reason is simply that the relationship between Japan and the United States cannot continue to be as amicable as it appears to be on the surface. There is an inevitable conflict between Japanese interests and American interests so long as the two nations insist on building their power to support their lifestyles and their profits and therefore set their priorities on war, rather than on a peacetime economy. People who are concerned with life and justice ought to express their views and demand that their governments overhaul their present warlike policies. Japanese imperialism can be checked only through the world opinions of peace–loving people. Without a policy that gives priority to the needs of the welfare of the masses and their enthusiastic support and involvement, the basic politico-economic issues and humanitarian problems cannot be solved in Asia or anywhere else. Such policy at this time is yet to be formulated.

Notes

1. V. I. Lenin, *Selected Works,* Vol. V (New York: International Publishers, 1943), p. 56.

2. Ibid., p. 58.

3. *Economist, Keizai,* April 20, 1967, Tokyo, p. 91

4. *Yomiuri Shinbun,* Morning Edition, February 25, 1969, Tokyo.

5. Tokusen Bunseikai Kenkyusha, *Nippon-no Tsukusen Kigyo,* or *The Monopoly Enterprise of Japan,* Vol. I (Tokyo: 1969) p. 87.

6. David E. Lilienthal, *Big Business: A New Era* (New York: Harper, 1953).

7. Keizai Chosa Kyokai, *Kinyu Kikan-no Toyushi* or *The Investment of the Financial World,* (Tokyo: 1969).

8. Kamakura Takao, *Nippon Teikokushugi-no Toyushi* or *The Present Stage of Japanese Imperialism* (Tokyo: Gendai Hyoronsha, 1970), p. 352.

9. Tokusen Bunseki Kenkyusha, *Nippon-no Tsukusen Kigyo,* p. 54.

10. Masamichi Royama, "Problems in Self-Defense—Japan Since Recovery of Independence," *The Annals,* Vol. 308, (Nov., 1956), p. 171.

11. Quoted by Halliday, *op.cit.,* p. 38.

12. Paul F. Langer, "Japan: New Problems, New Promises," *Headline Series,* No. 134, (March-April, 1959), p. 38

13. Martin Weinstein, *Japan's Postwar Defense Policy, 1947–1968* (New York: Columbia University Press, 1971), p. 110.

14. Halliday, *op.cit.,* p. 39.

15 The Taft-Katsura Agreement is a secret agreement between Japan and the United States made in 1905. In this executive agreement, the Japanese Prime Minister Katsura declared, "Japan does not harbor any oppressive designs whatever against the Philippines"; and Secretary of War William Taft accepted the Japanese position in Korea, stating that "establishment of a suzerainty over Korea by Japanese troops to the extent of requiring that Korea enter into no foreign treaties without the consent of Japan was the logical result of the present war and would directly contribute to permanent peace in the East." See Sunoo, *Korea: A Political History,* p. 196.

16. Takehiko Hayashi, *Kita Chosen-to Minami Chosen* or *North Korea and South Korea* (Tokyo: Simul, 1971), p. 192.

17. Ibid, p. 188.

10 Epilogue

When the newly organized giant, New Japan Steel Company, decided to sell 100 million shares on the foreign market in 1970, a recent trend had been initiated among the Japanese financial giants.

It is true that 100 million shares consisted of only about 2.7 percent of the total shares of New Japan Steel Company. Nevertheless, the company had moved into the financial world as a world corporation rather than remaining a Japanese corporation. Most of the Japanese financial giants have been slow to encourage foreign investment in spite of government support. But direct loans to foreign governments by the Japanese government have surpassed private loans and investments since 1965.

In other words, public funds from Japan helped to stabilize political order among some underdeveloped nations. Private investments by Japanese companies have played a secondary role in those countries. In view of such a development, it was a significant movement for New Japan Steel Corporation to initiate such a process and identify itself as a multinational corporation. The intention is clear. New Japan Steel Corporation will intensify its competition in search of markets and raw materials with the rest of the steel giants like United States Steel and other American corporations.

Major Threat to America

It is abundantly clear now that Japanese industrialists will be, if they aren't already, the major competitors of American industrialists. Japanese industrialists have an advantage today over the Americans since the zaibatsu dominate politics and the central government. Under such circumstances, the Nixon administration's inclination to help business interests as opposed to wage-earners in order to combat Japanese competition was inevitable. As the international competition intensifies, the federal government will attempt to control more of the people's livelihood under the rubric of preserving the free enterprise system. Ironically, the more the government tries to preserve free enterprise, the more it will eventually destroy it.

The original intention of Japanese aid to numerous countries, including India, Pakistan, Ceylon, Taiwan, Malaysia, Thailand, Burma, the Philippines, Indonesia, and South Korea, was to prevent bringing about any kind of socialistic government, especially when economic aid also began to arrive from the socialist countries in 1954. It is true that the amount of this economic aid to underdeveloped countries was no more than 5 percent of the total amount of aid that came from the nonsocialist countries, 1954–1968. Nevertheless, the idea of socialist countries' involvement in the development of these Third World nations was deemed a threat to the policy-makers of Washington and Tokyo.

As a result of American encouragement, Japan has done her assignment well. She now controls economically the entire area of Southeast Asia and South Korea.

The economic relationship between these underdeveloped countries and Japan is now well-established. Initial government aid to these countries has been maintained, although the format has changed. They now purchase Japanese commodities with Japanese loans, develop their economy as Japanese junior partners, and prepare to meet Japanese financial investments in every aspect of economic activities.

In other words, these underdeveloped countries are totally

dependent on foreign capital, with Japan as their prime source. For instance, in the case of South Korea:

> In 1957–58, grant aid came mainly from the United States. By 1967–1968, commercial imports with Korea's own exchange covered two-thirds of the total and foreign loans accounted for 17.6%. A significant proportion of the loans and some of the giant aids came from Japan and could be used only for purchases from that country. But, more important, Korea was able to use its own foreign exchange to buy from the lowest cost source, and for many commodities this source was Japan.

Another important aspect of these economic relationships is that Japan, while financing industrial development in South Korea and other Asian countries, also discourages them from competing with Japanese goods in Japan. There are hardly any Korean manufactured goods in Japan today. Most Korean commodities have replaced Japanese goods in the United States, while Japan is shifting its concentration to heavy industries.

What will happen to Japanese investments in these countries if the people of these nations begin to fight against Japanese imperialism? Risk is there. Every one of these countries has had previous experience with Japanese imperialism and Japan is probably not one of the more popular countries they would like to associate with, in spite of her economic aid. To prevent any such anti-Japanese movement, Japan has already been supporting political regimes whom she can trust. Not only that, several political leaders like former Prime Ministers Yoshida, Kishi, and Sato have expressed the view that countries like South Korea are very important to Japanese national security.

The implication is quite clear. Japan may interfere with military force in South Korea or any other place to protect her national interests. Consequently, Japan is building up her military force with the complete understanding and help of the United States. Again, we are witnessing the multinational nature of imperialism, and exploitations will continue in those countries by multinationalistic imperialism, until the competition intensifies among the imperialistic powers themselves.

Is Conflict Inevitable

When will such a conflict among the powers—especially between Japan and the United States—be intensified? American military involvement in Asian countries, except China, North Korea, and North Vietnam, is a well-established fact. With such predominant control over these small nations, why does the United States continue to allow Japan to dominate these countries economically? As pointed out elsewhere, Japan controls most of the markets that used to be American. For instance, the amount of Japanese exports to Southeast Asia has increased more than twice from 1965 to 1969. In 1965, her exports to the region amounted to about $2 billion, but increased to $4.5 billion in 1969. American policy could easily change such a trend. Japan could not penetrate her commodities into these regions without American support. As a matter of fact, it was an American policy that encouraged Japan to move into these areas with dynamic force. In 1969, Japanese firms invested about $57 million and employed about 20,000 workers in Thailand. This was done not only to take advantage of the low wages of workers, which attracted Japanese investments, but also the political stability of the country was an important factor for the foreign investors.

What happens when an anti-Japanese movement occurs as happened in the Philippines in the 1960s? In the case of the Philippines, President Marcos' administration decided to take strong measures to suppress any such patriotic movement and created an absolutist regime. Such happenings are common among the underdeveloped nations when the political leaders are anxious to attract foreign capital to develop their economy.

It becomes obvious that Japan will do everything possible to support such regimes and might even give military aid to these countries, patterned after the American involvement in South Korea and South Vietnam.

Why is Japan so anxious to control these regions? Because Japan needs raw materials as well as markets in Southeast Asia. Major European and American interests are already dominating important raw materials like oil, timber, rubber, which she needs to develop her heavy industries. Japan started late and needs to catch up. For instance, in 1970, Japanese firms invested about $7 million in iron ore, fishing, and timber business in Indonesia. Such aggressive policy in the development of natural resources will inevitably create ill feelings between the Japanese and the indigenous people.

The possible conflicts between the Japanese and the indigenous peoples of these areas are rather minor problems compared to the possible conflicts between Japan and the United States.

Japanese commodities have already created a major economic controversy in the United States in the last decade or so. Very few Americans realize that American tuna industries on the West Coast closed up their business due to Japanese imported tuna. Not many Americans know that the silk industry in New York is in trouble and so is the entire textile industry, which Mr. Nixon tried to save through a political deal with Southern votes. Electronics and related commodities have had a tremendous impact on the American market. We expect further situations in the field of steel as well as in the automotive industry in the near future. Japan exports 30 percent of her total export goods to the United States, and 70 percent of them are heavy chemical items. This is only the beginning. There are many more items that Japan is anxious to export to the United States that are now prohibited. But how long will that last under the free enterprise system? Ironically, the United States imports Japanese manufactured goods while exports of her agricultural products go to Japan!

Japanese business firms are now actively engaged in new adventures in the United States. In order to safeguard their markets in the United States, many Japanese firms have already invested considerable sums in America. Under the liberalization concept, it is feasible to accept Japanese investments in the United States, while the American companies invest their surplus capital in Japan.

The leaders of Japanese firms in this field are Mitsui Petroleum Chemical, Hitachi Manufacturing Company, Wazumi Electric, Daito Metal, Aji-no-moto, Nisshin Foods, and Kanebo Manufacturing.

Combined investments of these companies in the United States were about $600 million by 1969. Again, it is clear now that the Japanese financial giants are eager to compete with

Americans not only in Southeast Asia, but on the American home front as well.

With such ambitious plans, Japanese financial capital will not play a subsidiary role in the future as it has been accustomed to under the shadow of America. It is no accident that the Japanese government with the support of the zaibatsu groups is now anxious to build up military forces.

The recent American dollar crisis in international financial circles probably enhanced the Japanese position of a stronger self-defense posture. The Japanese defense budget has been comparatively low in the past because of the American commitment in Japan. Only 7.16 percent or about 570 billion yen out of the total budget went for defense in 1970. Compared to other consumer goods or even heavy chemical commodities, the defense budget was low in Japan, especially when it is compared to the astronomical figures of the American defense budget. Such low figures do not mean that the Japanese defense posture is decreasing, however. Contrary to the figures, Japan has been steadily increasing her military commitment for the past decade.

Defense Spending Increased

Japan's military supplies have increased 11.3 percent during 1963–1968, while West Germany's only increased 2.1 percent, England, 1.2 percent, Italy and France, 5 percent each, and the United States, 8.7 percent in spite of the Vietnam war.

The increase in military supplies has stimulated armament industries in Japan. Once, expanded armament industries with heavy investments could not be reduced without financial sacrifices. These industries, primarily a few limited zaibatsu groups (due to large capital requirements and close political associations), were not willing to sacrifice their government-guaranteed profits. As a matter of fact, these industries were and are strong advocates of the self-reliance of Japanese defense. Once started, the self-defense posture will gradually change to national-interest defense posture. In other words, wherever they find Japanese commercial interests, they will claim the necessity of their defense. Their claiming of the South Korean market as part of the Japanese national security region is one example.

This claim of the Japanese industrialists is a natural result of Japanese monopolies. We may compare it with the situation of Vietnam. American armament industries earned extraordinary wartime profits during the Vietnam war. The Nixon administration had to negotiate a peace settlement with North Vietnam due to pressure from the American public. If peace comes to Vietnam, the American armament industries will face a drastic reduction of their sources of profits.

The Nixon administration, under the pressures of multinational corporations, as well as American workers, had no choice but to continue the war in Indochina. The war has expanded into Laos and Cambodia. The United States is unable to convert its wartime economy to a peacetime system because the federal government is predominantly under the influence of the American corporations and the military-industrial complex. The United States almost doubled her sales in arms for the fiscal year which ended in June, 1974. Sales amounted to $8.5 billion, and the United States remains the world's leading arms supplier.

The business circle, and to some degree even the working class circle, were horrified by the thought of changing the economic situation, an idea proposed by Senator George McGovern during the 1972 presidential campaign.

How can the major companies like General Dynamics, Lockheed Aircraft, United Aircraft, and Douglas afford to curtail their production when three-fourths of it is occupied with defense goods? McDonald-Douglas Company, producer of phantom F-4 planes, gets 75 percent of its business from government contracts. Eighty-eight percent of Lockheed's production consists of government contracts, and 67 percent of the production at General Dynamics is also from government contracts. In the total picture, one out of five working families in the United States receives paychecks through these armament industries. Moreover, these giant corporations are crowded with retired generals and admirals in executive positions.

In recent reports to the United States Congress, the Export-Import Bank reported that the Pentagon had arranged for the bank to provide a direct long-term low interest credit to Iran of $200 million in 1974 "for exports of defense articles and service."

Iran bought $4 billion worth of arms from the United States, but Iran has also earned billions of extra American dollars since the rise in oil prices.

High government officials speak freely of the arms program in terms of maintaining the American arms industry and labor market and earning balance-of-payment dollars against the new high deficits created by the current price of oil in 1973–1974. This program was encouraged by former President Nixon on December 20, 1973. President Nixon directed the establishment of an interdepartmental committee on export expansion, and has given full approval to an open-ended arms sales effort.

Similar conditions are now developing in Japanese industries today.

Nixon Doctrine

The American policy encouraged by the Nixon Doctrine advocated that Asians defend Asia with American economic aid, but without American troops. Japan is again building military forces to defend her interests. There are two basic domestic conditions prevailing that enhance the militarization in Japan. Japan, again with American encouragement, has expanded her economic activities among the developing nations in Southeast Asia. As pointed out previously, not only to secure markets and raw materials, but also to expand their capital investment in these countries, Japan initiated a dynamic movement after the declaration of the Nixon Doctrine in 1969.

Another important factor concerning the recent Japanese aggression in Southeast Asia is Japan's technological prowess. Japan is no longer dependent on American support in this area. She is self-sufficient in technical abilities, and she intends to surpass American industries in the near future. The Japanese government is ready to give full support to the development of highly sophisticated armaments.

Although it is difficult to separate politics from economic matters, it seems that Japan is concentrating more on economic causes than political ones in the development of armaments and building strong military forces. In other words, she will be more ready to defend her economic interests in Southeast Asian countries rather than trying to control them politically with her military forces as before. This is a distinctly different position from her imperialistic policy prior to World War II. One might even add that the neo-imperialism has a stronger economic appetite, and uses political means to achieve its goals. Japan has all the characteristics of neo-imperialism, in spite of her new constitution and the occasional ritualistic proclamation of democratic ideas by the government. Anticipating severe international economic competition, Japanese monopolists have already been advocating necessary public education and propaganda for the purpose of unifying the nation to protect their economic interests.

There are three basic problems the monopolists confront today in Japan. Due to rapid industrialization, there is a shortage of manpower. For instance, there were nearly two million steelworkers needed in June of 1969, according to the Department of Labor. The demand for high school graduates in the labor market was four times the total number of graduates in 1969, and the rate increased 4.5 times in 1970.

In order to solve the labor shortage, the monopolists are intensifying efforts to train the skilled workers by promoting them to a special elite rank among the working class. Such programs will attract some portion of the group, but will further alienate the other less skilled workers. It is a strategy of intensification of competition among the workers rather than enhancing the workers' welfare overall.

The second factor confronting the monopolists today is social disorder as a by-product of rapid industrialization. Due to the postwar Japanese economic "miracle," much like those conditions in America, the Japanese people became victims. The natural environment has been destroyed, the cities have been polluted, and human lives have been threatened.

Recognizing the seriousness of these conditions, the monopolists are appealing to laborers and the rest of the citizenry alike to help solve these problems. There are two implications in such an appeal. First of all, capital wants to share the blame with labor over such chaos, and the other is to minimize the conflict between capital and labor. Under the name of humanitarian endeavors and social services, the monopolists try to camouflage their wrongdoings at the expense of the workers.

Another problem the Japanese monopolists face is soaring

inflation. This is indeed a serious problem in international competition. To justify economic competition, the monopolists appeal to labor to sacrifice wage increases and involvement in political movements. In the name of patriotism and nationalism, the monopolists try to convince the workers that Japanese business, i.e., the Japanese national interest, depends on such cooperation between capital and labor.

Nationalism on Upsurge Again

The revival of nationalism and militarism is much like that of the 1930s.[2] The danger is not as imminent now as during the 1930s, because there are well-organized trade unions with membership numbering over eleven million, progressive intellectuals, the mass media; the Socialist Party, the Democratic Socialist Party, the Komeito Party, the Communist Party; and other democratic forces which challenge the revival of militarism in Japan.

Recently, a Japanese district court ruled that the Japanese National Defense Forces were unconstitutionally maintained. Judge Shigeo Fukushima of the District Court of Sappora, Japan, announced in his ruling, "Ground, maritime, and air Self-Defense Forces, in light of their size, equipment, and capabilities, come under land, sea, and air forces, mentioned in the second provision of Article 9 and are unconstitutional."[3] Judge Fukushima referred, of course, to the renowned Article 9 of the Japanese Constitution.

It was the first court decision on the issue of the constitutionality of the Self-Defense Forces, which has been one of the major legal and ideological struggles between peace-loving citizens and the war-makers in Japan. The struggle is only the beginning. The powerful war-makers are not going to yield easily. Every single prime minister of the past has promoted build-up of military forces in the name of national security, and the government, as long as it is under conservative domination, will defend its "right" to build the military forces.

To maintain peace and prosperity in Asia and the world, the American people must ally with the democratic forces of Japan, rather than supporting the monopolistic zaibatsu-dominated groups. These monopolistic groups with their military orientation could well become the major menace to peace in Asia and in the rest of the world.

People all over the world who want to maintain peace must be alert and check the revival of militarism in Japan.

Notes

1. David C. Cole and C. Lyman, *Korea Development: The Interplay of Politics and Economics* (Boston: Harvard University Press, 1971), p. 132.

2. Japan's Fourth Defense Plan for 1972–1976 had a budget of about $22 billion or more. Japanese emphasis is on the expansion of her naval force with an astronomical figure of $10 billion; the rest of the budget goes to the army and the air force. Japan is already producing jets and missiles at the Kawajaki Heavy Industry and the Mitsubishi Heavy Industry.

3. Richard Halloran, *New York Times,* September 8, 1973.

Index

About the Author

Dr. Sunoo is Professor of Asian Studies at the City College of the City University of New York. Korean born, he received his education in Korea, Japan, the United States, and Europe. He has taught at the universities of California (Berkeley) and Washington (Seattle), at Charles National (Prague), and at Central Methodist College (Fayette, Missouri),where he holds the E.M. Frank Professorship of Political Science.

The author of several books in English and Korean, Dr. Sunoo offered the first comprehensive Korean language and history studies in the United States at the University of Washington in 1943. While living in Seoul, he was editor of the Korean Review and editor-in-chief of the Korean World, an English-language daily.

Dr. Sunoo, now a U.S. citizen, is married and has two sons.